EMBRACING LOVE

my journey to hugging a
man in his underwear

by nathan albert

Read The Spirit Books

an imprint of
David Crumm Media, LLC
Canton, Michigan

For more information and further discussion, visit
http://nathanalbert.com

ISBN: 978-1-942011-29-3
Version 1.0

Cover design and photo by Jeffrey Bondorew. "Hug" photo by Michelle Gantner at Maladjusted Media. Used with permission.

Published By
Read The Spirit Books
an imprint of
David Crumm Media, LLC
42015 Ford Rd., Suite 234
Canton, Michigan, USA

For information about customized editions, bulk purchases or permissions, contact David Crumm Media, LLC at info@DavidCrummMedia.com

TABLE OF CONTENTS

ACKNOWLEDGEMENTS & ENDORSEMENTS

FOREWORD by andrew marin **XIII**

INTRODUCTION: what truly matters **XVI**

CHAPTER ONE: hugging a man in his underwear **1**

CHAPTER TWO: belong, believe, become **24**

CHAPTER THREE: getting to know people **36**

CHAPTER FOUR: how do we read the six main passages? **60**

CHAPTER FIVE: re-humanizing god's people **91**

CHAPTER SIX: holy moments **109**

CONCLUSION: the time is now **136**

RECOMMENDED READING **146**

ENDNOTES **154**

DEDICATION

To Tristan and my countless friends and loved ones within the LGBTQ community. Thank you for showing me radical love, the beauty of acceptance, and rivers of grace.

ACKNOWLEDGEMENTS

Writing this book has been surprisingly terrifying yet incredibly encouraging. I must express gratitude to those prophetic voices God used to encourage me to write this book long before I thought I could or had anything worth saying: Mrs. Washington, Austin, Ginny, and Dominique are a few of those voices.

I am so grateful to David Crumm, John Hile, and Dmitri Barvinok at Read the Spirit Books and Front Edge Publishing. You have, quite literally, rescued me. Thank you for bringing this project to completion. To Christina Faison and Allison Armerding, who turned my words into a readable book, gave me the motivation to keep writing, and allowed me to use the Oxford comma. To Carla Pratico, your work, passion, and love for God. To Jeffrey Bondorew, for your design of the cover and friendship.

To all those in the Evangelical Covenant Church, North Park Theological Seminary and University, University Ministries, New Community Covenant Church, Christ Church, and The Marin Foundation. It was in these communities where I was able to ask questions, doubt, learn, and experience Christ in fresh ways.

To Judy Peterson and Peter Hong. God has used both of you, more than any other pastors, to transform me into the pastor I am today. Thank you for being faithful to Christ, impacting God's kingdom, and training up the next generation of pastors.

To those who endorsed this book, I thank you for believing in this project. To all who generously donated to our Indiegogo Campaign to get this book into your hands, you made it happen.

To Andrew Marin for writing the Foreword. Without you and your friendship, Andrew, this book would not have been written.

To my dearest friends and family, including those within the LGBTQ community, who never gave up on me, who are better friends than I am, thank you for showing me love and making me feel like I belong. You know who you are.

To my family, Denise, Darryl, Amy, and Nellie. You are the best family a person could get. Your support, encouragement, and love have made me who I am. Life is always better when you are around.

Finally, to Kate, who loves me in ways I've always wanted but never knew I needed. Thank you for saying yes to life together. I am, and Foster will be, a better person because of you. Always and always.

ENDORSEMENTS

"Nathan Albert joins a growing number of thoughtful evangelical Christians who simply love LGBT people with deep loyalty and care. Nathan's love for those so long wounded by the church is not despite but because he loves Jesus. In this book he offers personal and theological reflections rooted in his own deep and wide-ranging experiences of being in relationship with LGBT Christians (and ex-Christians, driven away by the church). His is a significant contribution to a growing chorus of voices calling both for loving inclusion of LGBT Christians and for an end to fruitless Christian arguments and divisions. Warmly recommended."

- David Gushee, Distinguished University Professor of Christian Ethics, Executive Director of the Center for Faith and Public Life at Mercer University, author of Changing Our Minds, Kingdom Ethics, and The Sacredness of Human Life

"Nathan Albert offers a fresh contribution to a contentious topic in this thoughtful and heart-felt book. The only way for the Christian community to move forward in discernment around sexual diversity is to live the questions. Nathan beautifully portrays the primacy of friendship as an invaluable moral category that is not only Scriptural, it is Christ-like. In company with such faithful people as Pope Francis, Nathan reminds us that indeed the Spirit is able to do a new thing in our midst."

- Michelle A. Clifton-Soderstrom, Professor of Theology & Ethics, North Park Theological Seminary

"As the Campus Pastor at an Evangelical University I am so grateful for an additional pastoral resource as I care for the daughters and sons of our churches who are both gay and Christian. As we wrestle together may we become the answer to Jesus' final prayer "that we may all be one so that the world will know that Jesus truly is the Son of God" (John 17:20-21)."

- Pastor Judy Peterson, Campus Pastor, North Park University

"Nathan has wisely addressed the fact that the debate between homosexuality and Christianity is not going away and the church is losing its relevance within the broader community. Because of this, he has decided to do something about it! In his writing you can see his deep love and commitment to the Church without wanting to exclude the other; a powerful combination. His willingness to name his straight, white privilege makes this book, and his words, ones to heavily consider and allow the spirit of God to move in and through you."

- Candice Czubernant, President and Founder of The Christian Closet

"Into a Christian conversation sadly more often influenced by culture-war, ideological approaches than by the more excellent way of the Gospel, Nathan Albert offers a fresh way into the conflict–not around it: one led by love, prayer, and radical hope for an inclusive, expansive church of disciples of all sexual orientations and gender identities."

- Trey Hall, Consultant and Coach at Epicenter Group, Birmingham UK and former Pastor of Urban Village Church, Chicago IL

"Nathan writes from a place of gospel-centered love, challenging us to deeper hospitality and friendship with the LGBT community. Through personal narrative and sincere treatment of the biblical text, we are left reflecting on our own phobias – even our tendencies to simply proof text away God's image bearers. I'm grateful for a book that furthers this conversation, encouraging us forward with a posture of embracing love."

- José Humphreys, Founder and Pastor of Metro Hope Church, East Harlem, NYC

FOREWORD

I spent years with Nathan, sharing a tiny office for The
Marin Foundation in the basement of a church, witnessing firsthand his everyday commitment to the
exact words written in this book. What you are holding
is more than a book; it is the way Nathan understands
and conducts his relationships with those considered
the "other" by many in the Church. These pages con-
tain Nathan's outworking of Christian unity—the type
of unity Nathan genuinely believes Christ modeled for
all of humanity—as it applies to the divisive topic of
LGBTQ and faith.

Nathan is not here to make a case to convince
anyone his or her theological understanding is inherently right or wrong. Nor is he here to arbitrarily
deconstruct tradition while offering no way forward.
Nathan's aim is to seek, through Christ, the relational
and pastoral reconciliation that often gets lost in the
abyss of difference. Theological difference does not

define this work or Nathan's life, as unity is not defined as everyone standing in agreement when the last page is turned.

The path that led Nathan to write this book was that of a working stage actor turned seminarian turned pastor. And let's just say, this unconventional journey has led him to the experiences that perfectly situate him to communicate such a needed message of reconciliation. As you read this book, resist judging it by your expectations of who or what you want Nathan to be. This book is not going to be the exhaustive, be-all-end-all of written works on this topic. Rather, as I read this book, I came to understand it as Nathan's midrash. Turning each page, reading each story, and grasping the scope of his pastoral experiences within the cultural disconnect transported me back to that tiny church basement office where I and a bunch of our friends huddled around Nathan, listening to him inform our attempts to live a life of love.

This book was not written to make money or gain notoriety for Nathan. He is, as he says, just a pastor who happens to love his LGBTQ friends and colleagues. Thus, in these pages you will find Nathan pastorally addressing some of the most contentious ecclesial topics of our day: experiences of Christian youth coming out, State-sanctioned gay wedding ceremonies, handling congregational division surrounding homosexuality, and how to address LGBTQ persons attending your churches. Nathan will not give any reductionist answers to these points of contention. Nor should he. What Nathan does is something much more important. He invites you into his experiential frameworks for engaging the nuance of these topics, so you are able to prayerfully use his experiences as a springboard for your own theological and practical engagement.

Nathan is one of the most creative, artistic, and original people I have ever come across. I count it as an honor that he allows us into his life. Throughout this book you will encounter those who have shaped Nathan's life, theological worldview, and the intentional way he relates to all around him. His scholarship gives a direct and accessible overview of contemporary arguments; but more importantly, this book is infused with the lessons learned from the lives of real people, his friends.

I can honestly say that The Marin Foundation would not be what it is today without Nathan Albert. During his tenure as the Director of Pastoral Care for The Marin Foundation, I daily witnessed his sacrificial giving of time, energy, and empathy, even when he was running thin on all of it. Nathan poured the depths of his heart into countless hours listening to other people's stories—giving hope to those with no hope, showing love to those who had not felt any love in recent memory, and taking every second needed to make sure his brothers and sisters in Christ know who they are.

I am humbled Nathan asked me to write this Foreword, as I feel that over the years I have learned more from him than he from me. I sincerely hope you take your time reading this book, treasuring it for the legitimate expression of love, hope, and unity that it is.

Much love,
Andrew Marin
President and Founder, The Marin Foundation
(www.themarinfoundation.org)

INTRODUCTION:

what truly matters

Trevor[1] and I, both in our early twenties at the time, were up late after a performance of the musical we were in together. Our conversation had already run the gamut of interesting and odd topics when it somehow drifted to the topic of embarrassing piercings or tattoos. Having only my ears pierced, I could not speak as an expert on the subject. Trevor alluded to having a more embarrassing piercing, but was hesitant to reveal what or where it was. I barraged him with questions and guesses, and finally— perhaps thanks to the late hour of the evening or the additional beer Trevor had drunk—he showed me his embarrassing piercing: his belly button.

Trevor was the first man I knew with a pierced belly button, and he allowed me to give him a hard time for it. He even poked fun at himself for getting such a regretful piercing. Then, as the joking came to an end, Trevor asked me a question that gave our conversation an unexpected, serious turn.

"Did you know I was gay?"

"No, I didn't," I admitted.

Having broached this personal topic, Trevor plunged ahead and told me about how he came to realize he was attracted to men and how difficult it had been for him to let certain family members and friends know this. He described the difficulties of dating and his longing for friendship and companionship. Finally, he looked me straight in the eye and said, "Being gay is so hard. I didn't want to be born this way. I wouldn't wish being gay on my worst enemy."

Trevor's vulnerable words struck me to the core. Here was a man I respected as a friend and colleague, who possessed amazing stage presence, brilliant comedic timing, and witty sarcasm. His beautiful baritone voice always spoke to my soul when he performed. Yet as he bared his soul to me, I now saw how he ached to belong, desired to be loved, and questioned how life could deal him such a hard hand.

As I traveled throughout the country to work as a professional actor and singer at numerous regional theaters, I began to have similar conversations regularly. For whatever reason, the musical theatre world employs, and has become a warm community for, a lot of gays and lesbians. In fact, there have been times when I was not only the lone Christian in a theatrical production, but also the only heterosexual male. Thanks to my job, I became immersed in the broader LGBTQ (Lesbian, Gay, Bisexual, Transgender, Queer) community. I quickly befriended many lesbian or gay individuals, was introduced to bisexual and transgender people, visited gay bars, attended gay clubs or events, and generally became comfortable in that world.

Over the years, I developed a plethora of friendships that span a spectrum of sexual identities. Some of my gay friends are in monogamous relationships and some live in the often-stereotyped hook-up culture. I have also had friends who identified themselves as gay, but due to their theological beliefs are now in heterosexual marriages. On the other hand, I have friendships with gay individuals in heterosexual marriages who question if they should leave their family to pursue a monogamous gay relationship. Some of my gay friends are openly proud of their sexual orientation, but choose to be celibate due to their theological beliefs. Some friends, after coming out, have grown closer to God as they continue to understand the relationship between their faith and sexual identity. And my friends who are intersex, bisexual, transgender, or queer have really expanded my spectrum and destroyed the abstract ideas I once had.

These relationships have shown me that the topic of sexual identity, and orientation, is not a black and white abstract issue. Even the terms we use to describe a person's sexual orientation can have different meanings. Due to this, it can be difficult, and at times frustrating, to talk about this topic. We will discuss in more detail how defining, using, and associating such terms as "homosexual," "gay," "lesbian," among others can make conversation confusing. Yet, it is a confusing, beautiful, complicated picture created by a colorful community of people with diverse stories and experiences. In a world that would prefer this topic to be abstractly black and white, the more we learn about people in the LGBTQ community, the deeper our understanding and compassion will be, which can sometimes mean things get a little less black and white than we might hope or like. Fortunately, grey is often considered a neutral and safe color that is easier on the eye. When we venture into this world of grey, we will realize what was often an abstract issue really isn't an issue at all.

My Two Loves

For years, I was torn between two loves: my friends and the Church. I was raised in a strong Christian home and regularly attended church. We were a part of Bible studies, prayed together as a family, and served our community. In church, I grew to love God, learned that I was loved by God, saw people's lives transformed by God, experienced God in my own life, and found a community that welcomed me. In my home, I learned to love the larger Church—the Bride of Christ, as some people call her. I was taught that She's the hope of the world. I believe Her to be a beacon of light and hope to a world that needs refreshingly Good News. She was created by God to be a counter-cultural movement of people devoted to love, peace, justice, and mercy. I always wanted to be a part of a movement larger than myself.

At the same time, I loved my friends who happened to be gay. They accepted me, a heterosexual, and welcomed me into their community. I heard their pains, struggles, hopes, joys, longings, and frustrations. The ones I worked with in theatre became my family and closest friends. Yet sadly, I learned that a disproportionately high number of my gay friends had had horrific experiences in the Church; in fact, it seemed to be the norm. I was crushed to hear that my friend, Tim, for example, after serving in his youth group for years, was kicked out when he told his pastor he was attracted to men. Even more painful was hearing that his Christian friends literally spit on him because he was gay.

The more I learned about the LGBTQ community, the more I discovered that they did not feel welcomed in most churches. The more I spent time in churches, though, the more I learned it didn't seem as if they wanted to welcome my gay friends. Why could the Church I loved so dearly not welcome the friends I loved so dearly? Why could the friends whom I loved so much detest the Church I loved so much?

Sadly, I have seen these two communities behave in absolutely vicious ways toward one another. Witnessing what appears to be hatred and pure disgust in their eyes, I have heard Christians spew shocking, venomous words about LGBTQ people and same-sex relationships. We all are aware of Christians who hold up signs with names and words I am ashamed to say. On the other hand, I have also heard the LGBTQ community bash the broader Christian community and make countless jokes about the hypocrisy and ignorance of Christian men and women. LGBTQ individuals are just as guilty when it comes to speaking harsh and derogatory words toward Christians, God, and Jesus.

At the same time, I know there are many members of both communities who grieve the hurts and broken relationships on both sides, and are searching for answers, healing, and reconciliation. I have seen numerous Christian parents weep as they share how their children came out and do not know where to turn. Some even blame themselves for a friend or family member's orientation. Many Christians have become champions and the biggest supporters of their gay family members or friends. And while I have seen LGBTQ individuals be reconciled with their families or church communities, I have also seen countless LGBTQ individuals weep as they share their desire to be in a church community, to pursue Christ, and develop their faith.

My Hope and Aim

Incredible books explaining what the Bible teaches about homosexuality have already been written, many by dear friends and mentors. In this book, I don't intend to spill any more ink than is necessary to point out that there are some differing interpretations of certain biblical texts that deserve to be taken into consideration by every person who desires to educate him or herself on the subject. My primary concern is to address the fact that we are on a dangerous social precipice. An entire culture is fleeing the Christian community, feeding a movement that is denouncing God due to the mistreatment of LGBTQ individuals, constant dehumanization of a people loved by God, and Christian division and disunity. **I believe that if Christian communities do not live as merciful and compassionate men and women who pursue unity and reconciliation, then our discord, division, and disunity will cause LGBTQ individuals to give up entirely on God.** As much as it pains me to say it, I have a sneaking suspicion this is already happening much more than we would hope to admit.

People have often asked me why I am so passionate about reconciliation between the Church and the LGBTQ community. I remind them this isn't the only issue about which I am passionate. I am passionate about women in ministry, racial reconciliation, cultivating multi-ethnic churches, fighting personal and systemic injustices, forgiveness, minimalism, caring for creation, living as good stewards of all our resources, and more. But my passion about this subject is ultimately about love. I love my gay friends and family members dearly. I do not love them because they are gay; I love them because they are my family and friends. And because I love them so deeply, I am saddened that so many Christians refuse to show them the grace of God, which I understand to be a free gift God offers to everyone.

When my loved ones are refused fellowship with Christians in a church body, called dehumanizing names, or viewed as inherently evil, gross, or immoral simply because of their sexual orientation, I am angered. It grieves me that people I love so dearly are not welcomed to partake in something else I love dearly, the body of Christ and the fellowship of all believers. I want my numerous gay friends to be able to freely stand with me in a church worshipping our risen Lord together, but I wonder if and when this will happen.

At times, I get tired. I am tired that Christians spend so much time arguing over biblical interpretations and fighting to convince others that what they believe is true. I am tired a book like this keeps getting written, exhausted that Christians continue to speak in abstract theologies rather than seek to serve the needs of people in our community. Being viewed as heretical, out of touch with Scripture, watering down the Gospel, a wolf in sheep's clothing, or even questioned about my own sexuality is wearisome. I am tired that avoidance has become the manner in which we handle divisive topics. As we debate and fight over positions, we leave those we are called to love in the dust.

As I have ventured into the emotional and passionate discussion pertaining to homosexuality and the Christian community, I have found that there is often a lot of fear. There is fear about theological doctrine, fear that we are dismissing the authority of Scripture, fear that conversation will turn into an endless debate, fear of diminishing the severity of sin, fear of being uncomfortable, and so much more. The more fear I sense, the more I am reminded of the words of John in his first epistle, "There is no fear in love. But, perfect love casts out fear."[2]

It is time that we love one another so well that we have no fear. I want—actually, I need—to be so loved that I have no fear in voicing my doubts, failures, thoughts, and beliefs. Our LGBTQ sisters and brothers need to be so loved that they have no fear; it is cast out. Yet at the same time, I must love others so well that they have no fear about this topic. If we can love one another in a way that casts out fear, I have such hope for the Church and the Christian community. A love like that will unite us. It will remind us that we are the Body of Christ, the family of God, and a community of people that need one another. Wouldn't a community of people who have no fear because they love each other so well be wonderful? Wouldn't that be a community in which you would want to belong?

My goal throughout this book is not to divide, push people away, or convince the reader his or her theological understanding is inherently wrong. Rather, my aim is to unite. Christians must recover the importance of unity. It is a high calling; one where we must "out-grace" one another, serve one another, put others before ourselves, and love in a way that casts out fear. Yet, we are better when we are together. As I share my journey and story, I hope to remind us that when we divide, we are giving the watching world yet another reason not to be a part of the Christian community, not to hope that the Gospel is good news, and ultimately, not to believe in the triune God of love. As a pastor, it is my heart's desire to see people respond to the Good News found in who Jesus is and what Jesus has done.

I know I can only speak so much about the LGBTQ community and its history. I will never truly know what it's like to experience a same-sex attraction and be a Christian. Because of this, I encourage you, as I will throughout the book, to be in relationship with LGBTQ individuals. Learn their stories as you do life together. In addition don't only listen to my voice or other heterosexual Christian leaders, but hear those within the broader LGBTQ community. Some well-known voices that have impacted my life include: Jeff Chu, Justin Lee, Broderick Greer, Julie Rodgers, Eliel Cruz, Allyson Robinson, Brandan Robertson, Matthew Vines, Candice Czubernaut, Julia Serano, among others. Let their lives impact your own. It is what I did and it revolutionized my life. But hopefully, my story and experiences within the pages ahead can shed light for Christians who want to do better at having a conversation around this topic, whatever their orientation. Such conversations have been done so poorly and have rarely been dialogues. Instead, they quickly become heated, passionate arguments that eventually lead to name-calling and dehumanization. When we sacrifice relationship in order to be right, we have forgotten what truly matters.

1

CHAPTER ONE

hugging a man in his underwear

In high school, I dreamt of becoming a professional actor and singer. My senior year, I decided to earn my bachelor's degree in musical theatre performance. At the time, I did not know much about the acting world. One of the only things I really knew was that many theatrical actors were rumored to be gay.

I remember walking between classes one day and wrestling with whether or not I was fated to "turn" gay if I became an actor. When and how would it happen? Would I simply wake up and know I was gay, or would I choose to be gay? Intruding on these questions was the fact that as long as I could remember, I had liked girls. I was dating a girl at the time, and I really liked her. By the time I reached my next class, I was positive I was not gay. All my self-examination affirmed that I was indeed heterosexual, had always been so, and had even been born that way. Three minutes was all the time I "struggled" with my sexual orientation—a vast contrast to what many LGBTQ teenagers and individuals experience.[3]

Unlike many youth today, I had almost no exposure to openly gay people as a teenager. My only references for "gay" or "homosexual" came from my conservative Christian family and church community, my adolescent peer culture, and TV. My family was not the Bible-banging type, but I was taught traditional theological beliefs, including the beliefs that women should not be pastors, the city was dangerous, people chose to be gay, and many gay individuals had an overbearing mother and/or an absentee father. I heard Christian radio programs that spoke out against homosexuality and warned that gay marriage was harmful to society. In my church and at home, I was taught that homosexuality was not what God intended for humanity.

As for my peer group, I regret that I and a few friends did poke fun at the more "effeminate" guys in our theatre department and classes—that is, the guys who hadn't progressed as far through puberty as we had. We were not sure if they were gay, but because they had only befriended girls and were stylish dressers, we guessed that they were. Sadly, I participated in a social system that judged people by their gender expression or clothing choices, a system that ultimately dehumanized people because they were different. As I have learned of the number of LGBTQ teenagers who take their own lives because of mistreatment by others, I am appalled that I could have unknowingly contributed to such harm.

In contrast, my one TV reference for LGBTQ people in high school was largely positive. MTV's The Real World had just begun (in my opinion, the 1990s were the glory years of MTV), and was one of the first shows to portray the life of an openly gay man living with AIDS—Pedro Zamora. I was intrigued by his life and his commitment and love for his partner, Sean. I was also confused why there was such controversy around his life, and how so many could deem such a wonderful person to be evil, vile, or disgusting.

College and Musical Theatre: Gay Until Proven Straight

When I left home and entered college to earn my Bachelor of Fine Arts in Musical Theatre Performance, most of what I knew and believed about homosexuality was abstract. But my abstract ideas quickly began to unravel as I learned that many of my friends, colleagues, roommates, mentors, and professors were gay or lesbian. As these relationships developed, I discovered that many of my gay friends had great relationships with their dads and did not have overbearing mothers. Many of my gay friends confessed that they did not choose to be gay, but rather discovered they were gay. Even more surprising to me was that many wanted to deepen their faith, be Christians, or had grown up in a Christian community.

In no way did my gay friends ever try to recruit people to become gay or to hop on board with their "gay agenda," whatever I presumed that meant. My good friend and college roommate did joke, however, that he received a kitchen appliance from the gay community as a reward anytime he "turned" someone gay. (I always told him that he would win an entire kitchen if I were ever gay.) I even had hopes of dating a girl I had a huge stage crush on, only to learn she was a lesbian.

These were my friends, my gay friends, and I did life with them. The abstract became flesh and blood. The unknown became known. The false assumptions became untrue. "Those people" became my closest friends. Once I started working professionally in the world of musical theatre across the United States, I became immersed in the LGBTQ community. In the musical theatre world, men were considered "gay until proven straight." This didn't bother me. It was not an attack against my masculinity or my sexual orientation; it was simply a reality of the musical theatre world. It came as a part of the job.

One of my favorite reminders of this is a photograph I have framed. It's a still shot of the number "Nothing Like a Dame" from the musical South Pacific, in which a group of sailors sing of their longing for female companionship while stationed in the Pacific Islands during World War II. The photo shows a dozen men, half of whom are shirtless, all dressed as the epitome of masculine sailors singing about women. The comic irony is that the majority of the men in the photo could not honestly sing of their desire for a dame. They were definitely acting. For me, this picture encapsulates so much of what I love about the world of musical theatre. It is full of beautiful sets and wonderful costumes, actors doing what they love to do, and friends I love dearly.

During these years traveling the country and performing, I continued to develop deep friendships with gay individuals, and found that the LGBTQ community was one of the most loving and accepting communities I had ever known. Even though I was heterosexual, and had in my own way participated in the dehumanization and demonization of the LGBTQ community, I was welcomed into friendships, included, loved, and cared for in that community. It occurred to me on many occasions that Christians could learn something about what a warm and welcoming community looked like from the broader LGBTQ community.

The Nazi and the Christian

As my LGBTQ friends opened up to me, however, I learned that a disproportionately high number of them had had horrific experiences with either Christians or churches. I was ashamed to hear them relate how they had been told they could not be gay, were kicked out of their homes, asked to step down from any form of leadership at church, or had friends, family members, and even pastors who would no longer speak to them, all because they were gay. Tragically, the average gay person, especially in the musical theatre world, views Christianity more as a religion of condemnation rather than a community of compassion.

CHAPTER ONE

A friend of mine, Jeff, witnessed this firsthand. Jeff and I shared a dressing room while performing at a small regional theatre in the Midwest. After discovering that we shared a strong Christian faith and upbringing, we bonded over the months we performed together, sharing personal life stories and struggles.

Jeff eventually moved to New York to perform on Broadway. He later shared with me a somewhat hostile experience he had while sharing a dressing room with some non-Christian performers. Time in the dressing room is a great way to build friendships, invent fun ways to pass the time, and enjoy laughs as you change into costumes. In this particular dressing room, Christian-bashing became a normal topic of conversation, and Jeff actually found himself agreeing with his fellow cast mates about some of the hypocrisy they were pointing out.

Jeff grew particularly close to a cast mate named Dave. They developed a great working relationship and then a friendship. At some point, Jeff let Dave know that he was Christian. For this reason, he was taken aback when, during one of their shows about four months into their run, Dave instigated a session of bashing Christians, saying things such as, "All Christians are completely ignorant of truth," "I wish every single Christian would drop dead—the world would instantly be a better place," and "I hate Christians."

After the bashing session, Jeff pulled Dave aside and let him know that even though the critique of Christians was understandable, the harsh attitude was hurtful, especially since standing before him was a Christian and a friend. Jeff expressed his desire to

[handwritten margin note: Something or someone customarily vehemently dislikes]

continue the friendship. At that point, Dave squared up to Jeff and boldly said, "I want you to know your beliefs are <u>anathema</u> to me. Having you in this room is the same to me as if a Nazi were here."

Jeff felt as though his breath had been knocked out of him. When he shared this with me months after the incident, he could still vividly remember Dave's tone, body posture, and the way he looked as those words shot from his mouth. As insulting as it was that someone—especially a friend—would compare him to pure, unfiltered evil, it was even more astonishing for Jeff to realize that another Christian had hurt Dave so deeply that Nazis and Christians were all the same to him. Jeff shared how, in that moment, he had felt a rush of compassion instead of blame or a desire to become defensive. Instead of looking down on Dave for his harsh words, Jeff told me he blamed the Christians who failed to model Christ's love and acted in such a way that a relationship with God would seem impossible for Dave.

After this incident, Jeff felt he was called to love Dave in a radical way. For months, Jeff went out of his way to care for Dave, serve him, and show him God's love through actions. Slowly but surely, the relationship began to mend. **Jeff let his actions speak louder than any words he could ever say.** Being rejected by his family and hated by ignorant Christians was, indeed, Dave's past, yet Jeff focused on a better future that included a loving relationship with Dave, demonstrating that not all Christians are hateful and hostile toward the gay community. Jeff and Dave eventually went on to develop a strong friendship.

Stories like this, although extreme, are surprisingly normal. According to many of my gay friends, though Christians speak of love, acceptance, compassion, joy, and peace, most of the ones they've encountered have behaved as if those attributes did not apply when dealing with anyone who was LGBTQ. A large number of my LGBTQ friends have given up on God precisely because God's followers gave up on them. Christians did not look or act any thing like the God they proclaimed. So my friends joined the LGBTQ community and created the kind of warmth, acceptance, and radical love they should have been able to find in the Christian community.

It appeared to me that many of my LGBTQ friends sought to find a place of belonging, love, and acceptance. As a Christian, I believe that place is, first and foremost, the Church. But instead of being welcomed into the Christian community, they were kicked out or pushed away. As they journeyed alone outside of the church community, LGBTQ individuals found others who had similar experiences, became their own loving and welcoming community, and shunned the community that pushed them away in the first place.

As I learned all of this, I wanted to prove my gay friends wrong. I wanted to show them that even though Christians do not always reflect the God of love through their actions, the God of love is still worth knowing.

From Tap Shoes to Seminary

Along with my dream of becoming an actor, I always thought that I might one day become a pastor. On an almost yearly basis after high school, some random event or thought encouraged me to pursue the pastorate. For a long time, however, I thought it was better to ignore the small voice nudging me toward ministry. I had no experience being a pastor, so I reasoned I wouldn't make a good one. Plus, I really enjoyed acting—the lifestyle was fun, the money was good, and my career was taking off. Yet, despite my efforts to ignore it, that small voice got increasingly louder. Finally, out of curiosity, I looked up seminaries and even applied to one—North Park Theological Seminary in Chicago—just to see if I could actually be accepted. Sure, I could tap dance, but I had no clue if I would get in to a school that trains pastors. Besides, I didn't know many pastors who could tap dance.

Soon after submitting my application, I tore a ligament in my knee, which forced me to drop out of acting work. My tap shoes were officially shelved. As I was recovering from knee surgery, I received an acceptance letter from North Park and a call inviting me to make a campus visit. After I went to Chicago, everything from finding an apartment to scholarships, financial aid, and getting in classes that put me ahead of schedule fell into place right away, almost miraculously.

When I arrived at seminary, I assumed my fellow students had all had a similar experience to mine. I thought that every seminarian loved going to gay bars, was comfortable in the LGBTQ community, and had countless gay friends. I was sorely wrong. Instead, **I became the one who introduced my seminarian friends to my LGBTQ friends.**

In seminary, countless people wondered if I was gay—not because of my orientation, but because I wore pink clothing, had earrings, plucked my eyebrows, spent numerous hours with my friends at gay bars, and was the classic "metro-sexual." Various friends and acquaintances reported that they had heard people talking about me behind my back and asking if I was gay. Some mentioned a particular lady who refused to discuss dating me because she thought I might be gay.

Now, people had been asking if I was gay for years. In the musical theatre bubble, I was judged gay by common association. But in the Christian bubble some people judged my sexual orientation by nothing but my seemingly "gay expression"—my clothing choices, hand gestures, or lack of masculine aggression. Because I did not fit into certain people's socially constructed, often conservative, understanding of gender, I was suspected or assumed to be gay. Sadly, many of my friends in the Christian bubble were making judgments and assumptions they had no right to make. All of this made me feel as if people were not really interested in me, but interested in whether or not I was attracted to men, which would ultimately label me as someone to be included or excluded.

Throughout seminary, I developed friendships with individuals planning to become pastors. They believed they had a call upon their lives to share the Gospel message to the world around them. Some of them had left lucrative careers to pursue seminary, some were starting their second or third careers, some were recently out of college, and some were retired and simply wanted to learn. A handful of these students wrestled with their sexual orientation. Some "struggled with homosexuality" and felt called to pursue celibacy. Others were in gay relationships for a season. Others wanted to pastor as openly gay individuals. They all felt called to pastor, to shepherd God's people, to proclaim the message of grace and truth, to baptize and give communion, and to do justice, love mercy, and walk humbly with God.

While I was in seminary, I began adapting my class assignments to study this fascinating topic and flesh out my thoughts about it. All that I was reading, experiencing, and thinking culminated in a thesis and other publications. A professor of mine read a paper about my experience with the LGBTQ community and told me that a lot of what I had written correlated well with the mission and work of The Marin Foundation, a non-profit in Chicago that seeks to build bridges between the LGBTQ community and the Christian community through intentional gatherings, scientific research, and educational forums. After meeting and developing a friendship with the founder, Andrew Marin, I decided to join their staff as the Director of Pastoral Care and Counseling. In that role, I developed even more friendships and connections with the LGBTQ community, intentionally lived in an LGBTQ neighborhood, provided pastoral care for hundreds of LGBTQ individuals, and began seeking reconciliation. I also participated in numerous Gay Pride Parades.

CHAPTER ONE

How a Hug Changed My Life

Every year, hundreds of thousands of people attend the Chicago Gay Pride Parade. The parade, one of the largest in the country, includes floats from different businesses and organizations, numerous LGBTQ groups marching, families and friends of LGBTQ individuals showing their support, and even politicians and celebrities in attendance. Before I attended the parade, I assumed it wasn't a family-friendly event due to the amount of drinking, nudity, or lewd behavior. However, I discovered it was not that at all. Sure, there were those who drank to excess or displayed their physical affection with their loved ones, but I had seen worse at sporting events, on reality television, or in a bar on a Friday night.

I also learned that every year, a group of Christians gathered to protest the Pride Parade at the end of the parade route. Someone pointed them out to me. They were standing behind a police barricade (for whose protection, I am not sure), holding signs and yelling verbal messages of dislike and judgment.

The first time I attended the parade, one of the gentlemen behind the barricade stood on a ladder with a megaphone unrelentingly yelling, "Sick, sick, sick, sick, sick, sick!" In that moment, I realized these men and women embodied 1 Corinthians 13:1: "If I speak in the tongues of humans or angels, but do not have love, I am only a resounding gong or a clanging cymbal." It was apparent to me that such loud cymbals and noising gongs repudiated individuals at the parade. Obviously, people didn't find their noise a melody worth singing.

I felt a desire to talk with this man shouting in a megaphone. I wanted him to know that I was a Christian, too. I wanted to learn why he had decided to protest the parade. As I snuck behind the policemen in front of the barricade, I spotted another older gentleman who wasn't as vocally active on a megaphone. I introduced myself and asked if I could speak to him. After he nodded, I asked him if he thought his method was working and if anyone had repented or was saved while he was there. He mentioned that he did not know of anyone who had repented. I asked him, then, if his method was truly working. Before he could reply, the man who seemed to be the leader of the group interrupted our conversation and threatened to have me arrested for harassing his group. This caught me off-guard—I felt they were doing more harassing than I had been. I explained that I was a Christian like him, was in seminary, and simply wanted to know why they were there. He ignored my question and responded with a rant about why I obviously had fallen away from God, should be ashamed of myself as a soon-to-be pastor, and deserved to go to hell for being at such a parade. It took all my willpower not to raise my voice or respond in jest or anger. When he picked up his megaphone and started shouting that any pastors at the parade would be going to hell, I decided to bid them farewell.

In 2010, a group of us from The Marin Foundation decided it was time to present a different Christian voice than the one everyone knew would be waiting behind the barricade at the end of the parade. One of our staff, who happened to be gay and my roommate, came up with the idea to do a public apology at the parade. We brainstormed the "I'm Sorry" Campaign, hoping that our simple action would show tremendous love. Before the parade, we made shirts with the words "I'm Sorry" on the front. We also made large posters with statements such as, "I'm sorry for the way the Church has treated you," "All humans have dignity," "I'm sorry for how I've shunned you," and my favorite, "I used to be a Bible-banging homophobe, sorry."

The day of the parade, the 20 of us met outside the local IHOP and staked out our place in the middle of the parade route. For the most part, we didn't know what to expect. We didn't have a speech planned if people asked us why we were there. We didn't have a large agenda. We simply held up our signs and enjoyed one of the country's largest parades. Little did we know what an impact an apology would make.

Some people walked over and gave us hugs when they saw our signs and shirts. Some shed tears as they embraced us. Others shook our hands and said thanks. Some merely smiled as they walked past, and of course, some didn't really notice at all. But by the end of the parade we had been inundated with hugs, thank yous, and tears, and left astonished that there had been such a reaction. We couldn't help but believe that God was somehow present with and working through us.

I decided to share my reflections on that life-altering day on my blog, which at the time had a readership of about 14 people, consisting of my family and closest friends. I wrote a post entitled *"I Hugged a Man in His Underwear. And I am Proud."* Within the week, the post had gone viral. Here it is in its original form:

I hugged a man in his underwear. I think Jesus would have, too.

I spent the day at Chicago's Pride Parade. Some friends and I, with The Marin Foundation, wore shirts with "I'm Sorry" written on it. We had signs that said, "I'm sorry that Christians judge you," "I'm sorry the way churches have treated you," "I used to be a Bible-banging homophobe, sorry." We wanted to be an alternative Christian voice from the protestors that were there speaking hate into megaphones.

What I loved most about the day is when people "got it." I loved watching people's faces as they saw our shirts, read the signs, and looked back at us. Responses were incredible. Some people blew us kisses, some hugged us, some screamed thank you. A couple ladies walked up and said we were the best thing they had seen all day. I wish I had counted how many people hugged me. One guy in particular, softly said, "Well, I forgive you."

Watching people recognize our apology brought me to tears many times. It was reconciliation personified. My favorite, though, was a gentleman who was dancing on a float. He was dressed solely in white underwear and had a pack of abs like no one else. As he was dancing on the float, he noticed us and jokingly yelled, "What are you sorry for? It's pride!" I pointed to our signs and watched him read them.

Then it clicked.

Then he got it.

He stopped dancing. He looked at all of us standing there. A look of utter seriousness came across his face. And as the float passed us, he jumped off of it and ran towards us. In all his sweaty, beautiful abs of steel, he hugged me and whispered, "Thank you."

Before I had even let go, another guy ran up to me, kissed me on the cheek, and gave me the biggest bear hug ever. I almost had the wind knocked out of me; it was one of those hugs. This is why I do what I do. This is why I will continue to do what I do. Reconciliation was personified.

I think a lot of people would stop at the whole "man in his underwear dancing" part. That seems to be the most controversial. It's what makes the evening news. It's the stereotype most people have in their minds about Pride.

Sadly, most Christians want to run from such a sight rather than engage it. Most Christians won't even learn if that person dancing in his underwear has a name. Well, he does. His name is Tristan.

However, I think Jesus would have hugged him, too. It's exactly what I read throughout Scripture: Jesus hanging out with people that religious people would flee from. Correlation between then and now? I think so.

Acceptance is one thing. Reconciliation is another. Sure, at Pride, everyone is accepted (except perhaps the protestors). There are churches that say they accept all. There are businesses that say they accept everyone. But acceptance isn't enough. Reconciliation is.

But there isn't always reconciliation. And when there isn't reconciliation, there isn't full acceptance. Reconciliation is more painful; it's more difficult. Reconciliation forces one to remember the wrongs committed and relive constant pain. Yet it's more powerful and transformational because two parties that should not be together, and have every right to hate one another, come together for the good of one another, for forgiveness, reconciliation, and unity.

What I saw and experienced at Pride 2010 was the beginning of reconciliation. It was in the shocked faces of gay men and women who did not ever think Christians would apologize to them.

What I saw and experienced at Pride 2010 was the personification of reconciliation. It was in the hugs and kisses I received, in the "thank yous" and waves, in the smiles and kisses blown.

I hugged a man in his underwear. I hugged him tightly. And I am proud.[4]

This blog sparked a lot of conversation and probably even more heated debate. It was seen in over 142 different countries, quoted on countless websites such as the BBC World News, Huffington Post, Sydney Herald, and GLAAD, and the picture of us hugging Tristan circulated the Internet millions of times. It was viewed more than 16 million times on Buzzfeed's viral post "21 Pictures That Will Restore Your Faith In Humanity."[5]

In addition, the picture was named one of the best images of 2012 on Reddit and Imgur, as it went viral for a second time. Celebrities such as Kristin Chenoweth, Lance Bass, Elizabeth Banks, Christina Applegate, and Alyssa Milano also promoted the blog, picture, and the "I'm Sorry" Campaign. Countless bloggers such as Rachel Held Evans, Nicole Wick, Tim Schraeder, among others wrote in response to our actions. Since then, the "I'm Sorry" Campaign has occurred in 22 cities in 6 countries.[6]

The picture itself, which was captured by Michelle Gantner with MalAdjusted Media and is on the cover of this book, has been viewed over 134 million times online. In the picture are Tristan, the man in his underwear, along with Andrew Marin and his wife Brenda, and myself, barely visible, hugging Tristan.

Hundreds of people commented on my blog. Some praised our actions, while others questioned our reasons for attending the parade. There were gay or lesbian individuals, some Christian and some not, who argued that we were too late in our apology. Christians voiced their judgment that we had lost our faith. Of course, and most sadly, there were people who threatened and attacked our personal character and even our lives. One person even compared me to the Antichrist.

It was hard not to take a lot of the comments personally at first, but after numerous attacks on my personal character, it became increasingly easy to dismiss such comments as having no merit. The oddity of the social media world is how people will type words they would most likely never say to your face. Strangers called me horrific names and made judgments about me without knowing anything about me. It's one thing to disagree with my actions or even my theology. It's another to judge my character, integrity, and motivations.

Emails came from all over the world. Some simply said thanks. Some said they were moved to tears. Some shared entire life stories. My favorites were the ones that gave a glimpse of hope. One, for example, was from a 16-year-old in Ireland who had been ridiculed and bullied because she was a bisexual Christian. She emailed simply to let us know that our actions gave her hope that her faith could grow. There were numerous similar emails from young teenagers and college students who found a glimmer of hope in what appeared to them to be a dark tunnel.

A few days after the post became popular, my dad called to tell me he had heard a Christian radio program read my blog post and discuss their thoughts on our actions. I listened to the broadcast the next day. They had people call into the show to give their reactions to the post or to anyone planning to do a similar public apology. As they had not asked me if they could discuss the post or interview me, I contacted the host of the radio program to mention my willingness to talk in person or on air about the post. The host stated that he appreciated my spirit and would consider reaching out further down the line. However, it was decided that talking with me on air was not the point of the show.

After the blog went viral, a gentleman contacted me to say that he was the man in the picture in his underwear. We communicated back and forth for some time. I eventually asked him if he would mind sharing a part of his story and experience. Specifically, I wanted to know what he would say to the Christian community. He told me that he was an atheist and wondered how faith was a part of his life, if at all. Tristan wrote the following email to me:

The openness and love that is shared on Pride Day is overwhelming and amazing to me. The fact that so many people who have but one thing in common can come together in such a united way and show love for one another is just mind-blowing. I noticed your shirts and was quite curious as to what you were all sorry about on such a celebratory day. When I read your signs, I must admit that I was taken aback by what they said. I have been judged and persecuted as a person and as a community for so long by so-called "Catholics" and "Christians."

I have been a victim of a hate crime and brutalized by four men in a bathroom. People have tried to make me feel as though I am less than others because of who I am. Just your signs alone made my entire Pride even more worth it for me. I was overcome with that warm, loving feeling from the crowd of people that you were with. The Marin Foundation along with its acceptance and ability to embrace gay men and women is why I came over to share an embrace with all of you. I hope that the world learns to grow and love from experiences and acts of kindness such as the one you exhibited on Pride 2010!

I was raised Catholic. I was an altar boy who went to church sometimes more than once a week. I was enthralled with the Bible and "the word of God." I then read the Bible cover to cover and saw so much hate, arrogance, and oppression, so I started to ask questions. The blatant disregard for human life and especially for women was just appalling to me. The more answers I received from my priest and other people of religion just became too much for me. So then, around age 16, I "lost my faith." I searched for a couple of years and looked into other beliefs just to come to the same conclusion. I practiced Zen Buddhism for a few years and started reading more into the universe and science. I then realized that I was just an Atheist and have been for over ten years now. I feel that people have the right to their own beliefs and their own lives, and should do whatever is in their power to be happy in this life. If I could say anything to the Christian community, I would say people must heed their own warnings and advice. Please learn to love as much as you have been taught to love. Realize that hate begets hate and that love (no matter in what form) is love! What are most of you so afraid of? To the others who have realized this, I applaud you! Please keep up the good work and spread your word and your love as far as you can. You truly are your God's people![7]

Like many of my friends, Tristan and others have given up on Christianity, and consequently God, because of Christians' mistreatment of gay and lesbian people. This should be alarming for those of us who love God's Bride, the Church. People view the Church and God through the actions of Christians, and for many, our reputation is one that repels them from both God and Christian community. **Yet people are longing and expecting Christians to look like Christ, rather than judgment**. They don't want us to have theological answers, be intellectually brilliant, or know all the answers. I think they want us to look and act like Jesus, plain and simple. As Tristan wrote, they want us to "love as much as [we] have been taught to love." For if we do, as both Tristan and the Bible say, people will know we are God's people. It's no wonder a hug can make such an impact.

CHAPTER ONE

Our apology at the Chicago Gay Pride Parade was never intended to make news, start a controversy, or even start a movement at Pride Parades across the United States.[8] We simply wanted to apologize to our friends. We recognized that our actions, and sometimes our inaction, caused people in the LGBTQ community to be hurt. And, if we truly believed that God created all people, and that they have inherent worth because they are created in God's image, then we needed to repent and apologize for the wrongs we had committed against God's children. Standing with signs publicly apologizing, though humbling, seemed the right thing to do.

Proud to Apologize

To this day, I continue to apologize to my LGBTQ friends when I hear their stories of pain, rejection, or abandonment. At times, it seems the first thing I can do. For some, though, an apology isn't enough and I understand that critique. Many people said to me our "I'm Sorry" Campaign was too late or wasn't enough. With so much past pain, it can be hard for people to accept an apology through words when it isn't backed up by actions. At the very least, apologies can clear the air and calm what is often a heated debate. At best, I think they have the ability to bring healing, hope, and reconciliation, which is every Christian's mandate.

Progress toward unity and reconciliation is hindered by churches that continue fighting over homosexuality as an abstract issue rather than upholding the humanity of LGBTQ individuals. Why would anyone want to be a part of something that is full of division and heated tension over "issues?" I have heard many Christians say that the "issue" of homosexuality is overbearing, that this "issue" is dividing churches, or that the "issue" of homosexuality won't go away. Yet, this is not an "issue" at all. This "issue" won't go away because this "issue" is about people. Have we forgotten this? When we try to rid ourselves of an "issue" by pushing it under a rug, we are ultimately ridding ourselves of people. **People matter. They matter to God, and they must matter to us.**

2

CHAPTER TWO

belong, believe, become

Remember elementary school? The line distinguishing the cool group and the not-so-cool group was clear—it was the line at the fold of the lunch table at my school. I always tried to sit as close to that line as possible. On days when someone was sick, I was able to scoot right up to the cool side.

In fourth grade, I wanted to be like the coolest kid around—Neil. That meant I had to swear a lot, so I did. I was a fourth grade sailor who cussed like it was my job. But my cussing career, and my dream of belonging, abruptly ended when my friend Patrick threatened to tell on me. I had to follow the rules.

During my freshman year of high school, I joined the cross-country team, which had won numerous national championships and was coached by an Olympian. I was short, a bit overweight, and could barely walk a mile under 13 minutes—but it was rumored that any freshman who did not join the cross-country team would be pelted with pennies as he walked the halls. So I joined the team—as a manager. Sadly, I could not even work a stopwatch properly. I finally surrendered my dream of belonging on the team and quit to audition for the musical.

We all have a story of searching to belong. We long to be part of a rich community where our needs can be met, where safety and security are free, where trust flows between each member, where we feel valued, cherished, and affirmed, and where we can flourish as human beings.

The Living Temple

I believe the dream of belonging was deeply instilled in each of us by our Creator. We were made for relationships and community. Yet, thanks to the legacies of sin, hurt, and brokenness, our quest for belonging is fraught with insecurity, difficulty, and pain. The thing we most long for is so often the most difficult to find and cultivate. The thing meant to make us thrive is so often the thing that wounds us most profoundly.

The Bible shows us that God is intensely interested in relationships and community, and has a long-term plan for restoring our broken relationships with God and one another. In the Old Testament, the plan was for the people of Israel to focus their community and religious life around a specific structure—first the Tabernacle of Moses and then the

Temple of Solomon—where God's presence was real and embraceable, and where healed relationships could be sought through learning how to keep the law and making sacrifices for their sin. When people desired to worship and encounter God, they went to these sites.

In the New Testament, however, we learn that God's ultimate plan was not for people to find God in a building, nor for restored relationships to be achieved through legalism or sacrifice. Instead, God made a once-and-for-all sacrifice for sin through the death of Jesus, the Son of God, enabling us to be reconciled with God so completely that God's very Spirit takes up residence within us. Thus, Scripture tells us, all who step into this reconciled relationship with God become "living stones" built upon a new foundation—Jesus, the Cornerstone—and "into a spiritual house to be a holy priesthood,"[9] a living temple where God's presence dwells. Now, people no longer have to go to the Temple to encounter God. Rather, God is brought to people through the people of God. As God's living sanctuary, Christians are to be the very presence of God in the world.

The watching world should be able to look upon the Church and see God manifested, an embodied presence—especially through how we demonstrate love and healed relationships. Jesus Himself declared, "By this everyone will know that you are my disciples, if you love one another."[10] The Church is not to be merely a club or social gathering we attend, but a brand-new culture where God's love, mercy, kindness, and grace permeate all that we do. She is the place where people should be able to come as they are to find love, acceptance, freedom, and a sense of belonging. Within the walls of the Church, the broken should find healing, the lonely should find fellowship, the doubting should find faith, the skeptic should find answers, the depressed should find hope, the unloved should find love, and the marginalized should find a family. She is the place where anyone should belong.

This is what we believe, at least abstractly. Countless churches have signs that say things like "Come as you are" or "All are welcomed here." But, when we get down to it, do we actually mean it? Do we believe that everyone should find community, experience belonging, and encounter God in the Living Temple? Do we truly believe that we welcome anyone into our churches, or do we have conditions?

In my own experiences with churches, I have found that acceptance is conditional rather than unconditional, and that the primary condition is behavior modification. Many churches and Christians follow an ecclesial model I call "Behave, Believe, Belong." People come into a church and are told they must behave in a certain way. They can't "drink or chew or go with girls who do," as the old slogan says. Once they are behaving in all the proper ways, then they are grilled about what they believe. They must believe the proper doctrine, that certain things are sin. They must know how to evangelize and be aware of churches watering down the Bible. Only after they behave the right way and believe the right things can they belong to a community.

Many of my LGBTQ friends have experienced the "Behave, Believe, Belong" model in church. Christians

27

have told gay people that they must first behave a certain way, then believe a certain set of doctrines, and only then can they belong to a church body. I know of friends who were asked to step down from volunteering in their church until they renounced their sexuality and committed to celibacy. Other friends were asked to leave youth groups they attended because they were gay. One friend could not be a pastor until he behaved in a way that reflected what the church wanted. For him, that meant he could no longer be dating other men, but instead, needed to be celibate. He was also encouraged to be quiet about his sexuality rather than open with any people within the congregation. Other friends have been pulled into offices for intervention intended to convince them their theological beliefs about homosexuality are incorrect and heretical. Far too often, LGBTQ people have been shunned from a community of belonging and blocked from encountering God in the Living Temple because they do not believe the right things or behave in the right way.

As it happens, "Behave, Believe, Belong" is the model most of the world uses as the basis for acceptance. Our places of employment, our educational institutions, and our parenting methods are all based on forms of behavior modification. One is rewarded based on her or his good behavior. It runs rampant in our culture, and it is no wonder that it has transferred to our religious culture. The problem is that the Church was not designed to function that way. In fact, I am a firm proponent that "Behave, Believe, Belong," is completely unbiblical and antithetical to the Gospel.

The Gospel Model

The message of the Gospel is "Belong, Believe, Become."[11] The good news of the Gospel is that, through God's sacrifice for sin, God has extended unconditional acceptance to sinners. God has opened the way for reconciliation and invited us into relationship with the God who is Love. Only when we enter through the door of restored relationship—into *belonging* to God as His beloved sons and daughters—does God lead us into *believing* in Him and *becoming* His disciples.

Those of us who have received this unconditional acceptance into the family of God are called to follow Jesus' example: "All this is from God, who reconciled us to himself through Christ and gave us the ministry of reconciliation: that God was reconciling the world to himself in Christ, not counting people's sins against them. And he has committed to us the message of reconciliation."[12] As ministers of reconciliation, we are to participate in creating a safe community where individuals can learn about Jesus Christ, the invisible God made visible. Only in this space of belonging will belief occur. And once men and women believe in Jesus Christ as Lord, it will only be through the work of the Holy Spirit that transformation—*becoming*—happens.

Belonging to a loving community where people can believe in God and this process is what enables individuals to become disciples of Christ. In the Christian community, God's process is known as sanctification. **There is freedom when Christians release control of**

how sanctification unfolds. The beauty of sanctification is that it is the Holy Spirit's patient outworking of radical grace in us, by which we become agents of reconciliation, change, and forgiveness, and participate in God's will on earth as it is in heaven.

The "Belong, Believe, Become" model can be seen in numerous passages in Scripture.[13] We see it, for example, in the life of the disciple Thomas. Thomas, one of my favorite characters in Scripture, belonged to a community for three years and was intimately known by Christ and the other disciples. Yet, Thomas did not believe Jesus was resurrected even when all the other disciples did. He declared that he would doubt the miracle of Jesus' resurrection until he was able to stand before the risen Jesus, touch His wounds, and put his hands in His side. Then, a week after the resurrection, Thomas saw Jesus face to face. Jesus approached Thomas directly and said, "Put your finger here; see my hands. Reach out your hand and put it into my side. Stop doubting and believe."[14] Once Thomas encountered Jesus, he professed and worshipped, "My Lord and my God."[15] Later, Thomas brought the Gospel to India. Thomas *belonged* to the community of disciples, *believed* after encountering the risen Christ, and ultimately *became* a martyr for his faith in Jesus.

The "Belong, Believe, Become" model allows people to be human. Belonging in community opens a space where we can feel safe and loved enough to display our struggles, openly confess our darkest secrets without fear of judgment, share our doubts, question our faith, and seek understanding. After all, every one of us experiences seasons and circumstances in which we doubt, just like Thomas. We are unsure, even when we belong to a community of faith. But eventually, we encounter Jesus. When that happens, we receive grace rather than punishment, love rather than a rolling of the eyes, and an embrace rather than judgment. Jesus did not yell at Thomas for his unbelief. Jesus embraced him with love and grace. This radically changed Thomas and was the catalyst for him to live a life fully devoted to Christ.

This text reminds us there are opportunities for us to act like Jesus. **Instead of passing judgment, we can extend grace.** We can be a community of Jesus followers who patiently stand with people as they doubt, wrestle with faith, and seek to live out their Christian faith. And when people encounter Christ within this beautifully loving community, it becomes easy for them to believe that the same kindness and love of God appeared in the person of Jesus Christ, and that God saved us not because of the righteous things we have done, but because of God's mercy.

This is the Good News of the Gospel. We do not have to have our act together and be perfectly cleaned-up, doubt-free versions of ourselves before we can belong to God's loving community. We can all belong as we are. Our deepest desires to be accepted, loved, valued, and cherished can be met without condition inside the Church. Once we believe and experience this, nothing can hold us back from becoming passionate followers of the God of Love. Once we embody this, our churches may bust from the seams with people longing to belong to community, hoping to believe, and finally becoming passionate agents of reconciliation.

Room to Breathe

The Church has warped the Good News of the Gospel by falling for the lie that our faith is about behavior modification. The "Behave, Believe, Belong" model that dominates so many churches turns the Good News into mediocre or difficult news, sending the false message that God will bless us if we obey, if we behave and believe rightly, or if we work hard enough. Frankly, behavior modification is exhausting. Who really wants to have their act together before they can find acceptance? Who really wants to be perfect before they can be loved, affirmed, and cherished? How is it good news to have your deepest desires met only after you have proven yourself as worthy?

Ultimately, behavior modification minimizes radical grace and emphasizes legalism and works. When people are forced to have their act together in order to belong, they often develop a distorted view of grace and God, and many give up on God entirely. It's no wonder people leave a place where they can't belong, and form their own community where they can be fully known and deeply loved. This is exactly what LGBTQ people who used to be in the Church have done—they have created their own "church" community where anyone can belong, be loved, be affirmed, be accepted, and be known.

In the wake of all the conversations stirred up by the photo and my blog in 2010, I felt called to open spaces in my home and church where the Gospel model "Belong, Believe, Become" could be practiced—spaces where, no matter their beliefs, people felt safe, accepted, were allowed to ask questions about Christianity, learn about the history of the faith, and even try to experience the faith to live as God designed them to live. In response to this call, I and another pastor from my church started a small Bible study for LGBTQ individuals. A spectrum of people joined the group—celibate, closeted, out and looking to date, and some in committed relationships for decades. We welcomed all of them. During our first meeting, we asked each person why he or she wanted to be a part of the group. As we went around the circle, we heard stories of people looking for community, others simply wanting new friends because of their loneliness, some wanting more knowledge of God and the Bible, and others hoping to find like-minded people.

The final gentleman who shared told us this was his first time in a Christian community in many years. After being shunned by church after church and burned by Christians because of his sexuality, he had all but stopped trying before he found our group. **"I've been looking for a place where I can simply be me and breathe," he said. "Tonight, I feel like I can finally be me and breathe."**

We never realize how essential oxygen is until we cannot catch our breath. So many of our LGBTQ sisters and brothers are longing to catch their breath, longing just to be themselves—themselves within the

How would one go about doing this?

Christian community. The stories I heard in my Bible study, and in my countless conversations with LGBTQ people, have convinced me that the Christian community and LGBTQ community are more of a family than we often realize. This is not an "Us vs. Them" debate. Many of these are stories of people who were raised within the church's walls, people who want to know God but have been ushered outside the walls of Christian community and blocked from membership.

You and I as Christians have the opportunity, and the mandate, to open our homes and our lives, move from abstract ideas about people to actually knowing them, and ultimately allow people to finally belong and breathe. Belonging—the first step in the Gospel model—is all about relationships. Just as God invites us into relationship just as we are, so we must learn to build relationships with one another. The Christian community must learn to be in relationship *with* LGBTQ individuals before we talk *at* them about our theological beliefs. We must extend to them the unique resource of the Gospel—that they have inherent dignity and value as those made in God's image, whom God has deemed worthy of God's sacrificial love. And we must remember that we *need* the unique reflection of God that they were created to reveal. It was God's idea that when God's endlessly diverse, dearly loved children gather into community, we will actually get a glimpse of who God is. Conversely, when people are not given the opportunity to belong to the Christian community, we all suffer and miss out on seeing the expression of God's imprint upon humanity. We see less of God.

I sometimes think our churches should be like a beautiful bouquet of flowers—a large vase bursting at the seams with different colors of the rainbow on the tips of green stems. Currently, many of our churches are more like a smattering of roses or tulips—all one color, all one size, and all one aroma. What happens when a lily approaches our bouquet? What happens when a hydrangea longs to be a part? They may feel they do not belong, that they are poor dandelions in comparison to so many roses. Who would blame them if they ventured off to find another bouquet, since they know they won't get what they need to thrive? Thus we are left with bouquets that aren't bursting out of the vase, rarely attracting outsiders, and lacking a rainbow of colors that fill a room with a beautiful aroma. Sadly, when all people cannot belong to our churches, we are not working the way God designed us to work.

3

CHAPTER THREE

getting to know people

Life is all about relationships." My father often said this to me growing up, but the first time I remember it really hitting home for me was when I became good friends with a cast mate, Mike, while working at a regional theatre in Tennessee. Beyond our love of Shakespeare, theatre, and dark beers, Mike and I were almost polar opposites. I was a professing Christian and, at the time, a registered Republican. He was an atheist and a registered Democrat. He was brilliantly intellectual and a self-proclaimed philosopher, while I was brilliant at not being intellectual and could barely spell philosopher.

Mike and I got in the habit of visiting a certain restaurant after each show—to the point where the wait staff knew our order: chicken strips, fries, and dark beer. Every night over our bar food, we discussed life, faith, and politics—every topic a Christian and an atheist should probably not be discussing, especially in a bar. Through our hours of conversation and calorie-consumption, we learned why we believed what we believed, how we came to our individual faith, how we voted, and our passions in life. One night after a long conversation, we returned home and I headed for bed. Just before I turned out the lights, Mike came to my room and stood in the doorway.

"I hope you know that I will never argue with you about your beliefs," he said. "I'll never fight you about them. You actually live what you believe, and I respect that."

I wanted to respond with an intellectual response that would make Mike proud, but it was late and I was full of chicken strips. I think I just said, "Ditto." Mike bid me goodnight, and I rolled over in bed and thought of my dad's words. Just before I fell asleep, I said them aloud: "Life is all about relationships."

Everything changes when we form deep relationships with people who are different than ourselves. When we have no relationships, or refuse to have relationships, with people whose lifestyle, culture, affiliations, or beliefs differ from ours, it is too easy to succumb to all kinds of anti-social problems—fear of the "other," stereotyping, dehumanizing, superiority, slander, ostracism, oppression. All of these are blatantly ungodly. But relationships humanize us. They help us to locate the irreducible common value we all share and invite us to cultivate respect, empathy, understanding, and appreciation for one another. They lead us past the reductionist stereotypes and false assumptions into the complex, beautiful dimensions of individual stories, thoughts, and hearts. And only in the holy space where we feel safe to share our unique stories and perspectives with one another can a true connection and honoring exchange of our life messages take place. Again, this is where we can begin to breathe and belong.

Relationships take time and effort to build. Consider the work that full-time missionaries undertake in order to develop relationships with people who are very different than they are. Prior to stepping foot in the country, missionaries to Thailand, for example, will spend months learning about Thai history, culture, and customs, and taking introductory Thai language courses. Once in Thailand, the missionaries might spend an entire year simply living among Thai people, hearing their stories, learning the language fluently, and participating in Thai customs—all before they share one word of the Gospel with the Thai people. They understand that the Thai people's ability to hear and receive the message depends upon it being delivered in their language, in a way that honors their customs and avoids cultural *faux pas*, and by people who have proven that they are there to serve and honor their audience.

We should take the same approach to building relationships with the LGBTQ community. Before Christians even think about presenting the Gospel to them, we must learn their culture, their language, and what they might find offensive so that we can foster and preserve mutual respect. Unfortunately, those within the LGBTQ community frequently see

Christians saying or doing offensive things that hinder any possible interest in Christianity. Christians often make their voice and opinions heard before ever listening to the voices of the LGBTQ community or learning their particular customs. This move is particularly counterproductive because it only triggers the wounds of those who have been rejected by Christians and strengthens our reputation as being harsh, judgmental, and hypocritical. As we learned with the "I'm Sorry" Campaign, Christians will hit the right nerve for many LGBTQ people when they take responsibility to acknowledge the hurts that need to be healed and wrongs that need to be righted.

A Place to Start

One day my dad asked me how he could begin building relationships with LGBTQ people. One of his coworkers was gay, and he wondered how he could talk to him about the topic. The coworker was also Jewish while my dad was a Christian, so my dad naturally had reservations about discussing faith and sexuality with him.

I told my dad that when the time seemed right, he should ask his coworker what it was like to be a gay man working at their organization. I told him to simply ask the question and listen, rather than share his opinion. To my surprise, my dad actually took my advice. One day at the office, my dad initiated a conversation with his coworker. He pointed out that homosexuality was somewhat of a hot-button issue within Christian circles, which had made him curious to know what it was like to be gay at work. He asked his coworker if he felt supported or if he found it to be a struggle.

My dad's coworker ended up sharing about his experiences with my dad for over 45 minutes. As they concluded the conversation, the man mentioned that he and his partner had barbecues at their home and asked my dad if he would be interested in joining them for one. My dad accepted the invitation. They continue to be close friends and colleagues, often sharing text messages, sending one another pictures of family or friends, and eating meals together at work. Most recently, my dad's coworker mentioned how much he appreciated being included in "family" things.

From many people's perspective, these two men had every reason not to be in relationship. One is Christian and the other Jewish. One is heterosexual and the other is gay. Yet, in the course of 45 minutes, they went from being coworkers to friends. All it took was the humble and honoring question, "What is it like to be you?" This is the beginning of reconciliation.

Isolation and Internalized Homophobia

As I have heard countless gay friends respond to that question, I have learned about the depth of their emotions and desires, their experiences with internalized homophobia, the history of the LGBTQ community and the gay rights movement, and much more. For the rest of this chapter, I hope to offer you the benefits of my education in hopes that it will inform your conversations and relationships. In later chapters, I will also lay out some practical advice in how to handle conversations and provide spiritual care within such relationships.

First, it should be apparent that being gay is often quite hard, largely due to internalized homophobia, self-hate, bullying, loneliness, and abandonment. Currently, the average age at which someone realizes he or she has a same-sex attraction is thirteen years old, though they do not usually declare themselves to be gay or lesbian until fifteen.[16]

This is an incredibly long time for young people to wrestle with these discoveries on their own, especially in a time of life commonly full of anxiety, fear, and self-loathing. Rarely will teens immediately tell their families or anyone in a church about their sexuality. Many friends have told me years after coming out that they were so lonely because they were unsure of whom they could trust to talk to about their sexuality. In some cases, the first outlet they used for expressing their emotions was Facebook.

Hearing these accounts has fueled my passion for the Church to be the place where people can freely discuss such emotions without the fear of rejection or judgment. I have long believed that difficult conversations should freely occur within Christian community. I would much rather have students engaging these conversations within the walls of the church or the home than the walls of a locker room. Also, such conversations take boldness and courage. Encouraging and acknowledging this is very helpful in such situations.

CHAPTER THREE

The younger brother of a good friend of mine had the courage to come out to me while his brother was out of the room. Throughout our conversation, he shared with me his interests in certain hobbies, television shows, and activities that all related to the LGBTQ community. He shared stories about his interactions with guys to whom he was attracted.

Later that same day, my friend revealed to me that he questioned if his younger brother was gay. Although I knew more of the story, I simply told him that he should have an honest conversation with his brother about the subject, even if it was awkward. They ended up having the conversation later on and it went very well. Recently I caught up with my friend's brother and he mentioned the conversation went so well that he almost forgot about this story. His relationship with his brother and family is wonderful.

Many young people go through a period of internalized homophobia in which they fear their own sexuality. Finding that you are attracted to people of the same sex can produce self-disgust that remains for years. This poor self-image is only increased as many people are bullied and harassed to the point of suicide because of their orientation. Many individuals in the LGBTQ community have to spend years working to gain a positive sexual identity. Most gays and lesbians find it essential to move away from where they were raised, which is why there are such large numbers of LGBTQ individuals in major cities. In these urban locations, they can be included in the accepting gay community. Chicago's Boystown was the first recognized LGBTQ neighborhood in the country. Of the thousands of LGBTQ individuals who live in this square mile radius of a neighborhood, many have moved there to escape, find community, refuge, safety, and a space to live openly. Only after developing a positive sexual identity will they possibly consider returning to a religious community or rebuilding relationships with family members who have shunned them

Many gays and lesbians have told me that their sexual orientation was not something they chose for themselves. Likewise, almost all biographies written by gay and lesbian individuals claim that they were never attracted to someone of the opposite sex.[17] As these stories recount, their sexuality is a truth they discover rather than something they try to become.

I do not intend to get into the debate over whether or not individuals are born gay, or whether or not God makes them gay. Too often, that debate turns ugly and, quite frankly, mean. However, as I have read different scientific studies, encounter women and men who are gay, heard stories from friends, I honestly do not know. There is no conclusive proof one way or the other. Some day in the future we may know for certain, but for now I am comfortable in not knowing. What I do know, though, is that all people are fearfully and wonderfully made. From the beginning, God has called people good. Because of this, no matter one's orientation and no matter if people are born gay or not, I believe all people have inherent worth, value, and dignity.

History of the Gay Rights Movement

In addition to building relationships, Christians can learn about the LGBTQ community by becoming familiar with their landmark historical events. Consensus is that the gay rights movement began almost 50 years ago on June 28, 1969 at Stonewall Inn in New York City. This is considered the day when the LGBTQ community stood up against oppression. Stonewall Inn is a bar located on Christopher Street in the heart of Greenwich Village. While living in New York City, I walked by Stonewall Inn numerous times unaware the historic events that occurred there. If you don't know the history that took place outside this storefront, it's easy to overlook.

Stonewall Inn was a mafia-owned bar that quickly became an oasis for many closeted gay men and women. Due to the laws of the time, it was illegal for people of the same sex to display any affection in public, hold hands, and even dance together. At Stonewall, such actions were allowed. Because of this, the New York police department often raided the bar on the grounds that it did not have a proper liquor license.[18] Paid-off policemen would warn the bar of coming raids so no one would be arrested or publically "outed" for either the lack of a liquor license or any same-sex behaviors.[19]

On the evening of June 27, 1969, however, nine plain-dressed police officers raided Stonewall Inn and immediately arrested the doorman, bartender, and three transgender individuals. In response, people in the bar began throwing beer bottles, trash, coins, and even bricks at the police officers. Although the fight never got overly violent, the protest continued into the next day. A few days later, close to 500 people had installed themselves in the street, shutting it down entirely. After some time, police arrested some LGBTQ individuals and beat others.[20]

On the year anniversary of these protests, the gay community in New York City decided to do a commemorative walk called "Christopher Street Liberation Day March," which ended in Central Park with people of the same sex openly showing affection.[21] The walk became the first Gay Pride parade. Eventually, major cities throughout the United States held similar walks on the anniversary of the Stonewall Riots. Today, Gay Pride parades all over the United States commemorate these events that occurred in New York City almost 50 years ago. Today, many people, even some within the LGBTQ community, seem to have forgotten this history.

Another interesting and important event in the history of the gay rights movement is the removal of homosexuality from the *Diagnostic and Statistical Manual of Mental Disorders*. Prior to December 1973, the American Psychiatric Association (APA) deemed that homosexuality was a mental disorder. Treatment of homosexuality included shock therapy and other methods used with mental disorders of the time. When the APA voted to change their classification of homosexuality, it helped to humanize the LGBTQ community and legitimize their experiences.[22] It also enabled the LGBTQ community to respond to critics who believed that homosexuality was inherently evil or perverted.

Fighting unjust laws is another important element of the LGBTQ community. For many years, one could be arrested for holding hands, kissing in public, and dancing with someone of the same sex. Cities and states had different laws and ways in which they were enforced. Once arrested, these individuals would be forced to register as sex offenders and, at times, denied parole.[23] Even sexual encounters that happened between people of the same sex in the privacy of their own home were considered crimes, as seen in the decision by the 1986 Supreme Court case *Bowers v. Hardwick*. Until the 2003 *Lawrence v. Texas* decision struck them down, there were still 13 states that upheld sodomy laws as misdemeanors or felonies.[24] Today in several countries outside of the United States, gay men and women can be put to death because of their sexual orientation.

Most recently, marriage laws have drastically changed within the United States. During the process of publishing this book, our country has moved from 37 states honoring same-sex marriages to the landmark Supreme Court decision, *Obergefell vs. Hodges*, guaranteeing all same-sex couples the right to marry within the United States. On June 26th, 2015, almost 46 years to the day of the Stonewall Riots, the Court ruled in a 5-4 decision that the Fourteenth Amendment requires states to issue a marriage license between two people of the same sex as well as recognize any marriage that was licensed and performed out-of-state. This decision overturned the 1971 case *Baker vs. Nelson*, that ruled the denial of same-sex marriages did not violate the United States Constitution.

I have had conversations with Christian individuals who are concerned that the topic of marriage has moved from a theological conversation to a conversation about civil rights. It is good to remember that our LGBTQ brothers and sisters have been denied over 1,100 marriage rights that heterosexuals freely receive. In recent years, many of these rights have been advocated to LGBTQ individuals. As a Christian, I am a proponent that all people be treated equally and fairly in our country and am pleased to see some of that happening.

LGBTQ activism has been focused on proving to society that this community is not immoral or evil, but instead are upstanding citizens who share similar core values as the rest of society. It is always sad when humans created in God's image must prove themselves to other humans that they have worth. And as we build relationships with LGBTQ individuals, I think you can clearly see the uphill battle many people have gone through to enable this reality.

Terminology and Hospitality

Throughout this book, I have been using the acronym LGBTQ (lesbian, gay, bisexual, transgender, queer). Now I want to take a moment to define these and other terms a bit more. I realize that these terms might be new and even overwhelming for some readers. I can imagine a nonagenarian who has been in the church for the majority of his or her life randomly picking up this book, reading the following section, and perhaps being very confused and/or uncomfortable. However, understanding and adopting the terms in this section is an act of kindness and hospitality to our sisters and brothers, fellow human beings, who happen to have a different sexual orientation.

I realize that for some people, adjusting terminology might seem like a nuisance, or feel it is tantamount to changing their opinions or belief; however, this is not the case. Being respectful of certain terminology is not being politically correct, throwing away beliefs, or even dismissing the Bible. Rather, in a world with diverse people and experiences, changing language to accommodate others is a simple way to show politeness, hospitality, and kindness toward other people—something for which Christians should be known.

Lesbian, gay, bisexual, transgender, queer, and other terms are used by those within the broader LGBTQ community to describe sexual orientation and/or gender identity. Lesbian, gay, and bisexual generally signify sexual orientation—sexual attraction for the same sex or both sexes. At times, bisexuals do not feel included into the broader gay or lesbian community because they are attracted to both men and women.

Transgender is a term that refers to gender identity rather than sexual orientation. In the last few years, there has been an increased visibility of transgender issues and concerns, especially with the media's attention of Caitlyn Jenner. Transgender individuals are those whose gender identity and expression does not match their biological sex—for example, someone who at birth was defined anatomically and culturally as a male but who later identifies as a female. Usually this will involve taking on the gender expressions, include dress and behavior, of the opposite gender. Some transgender individuals may go through hormone treatments or surgical procedures in order to develop physical characteristics of their desired gender. Even with the help of trained medical professionals, this can be an arduous process and journey. Those men and women often label themselves as *post-op transgender males or post-op transgender females*. Transgender individuals can identify as heterosexual, bisexual, gay, or even asexual.

I have been a part of church communities where transgender men and women have been congregants. In my conversations with them, I often ask them what pronoun they would like me to use in referring to them. One particular individual told me he labeled himself a *transgender male* because he was biologically female but identified as male. (Others are biologically male but identify as a *transgender female*.) He shared with me his hesitancy to be a part of any gendered ministries. He did not feel as if he would belong to an all-men's gathering since he was still anatomically female, yet at the same time, he did not feel he could attend the women's morning small group, as he outwardly looked masculine. We discussed his identity, his fears, and his longings to find a Christian community that would foster his faith.

One term that is being used more regularly is *cisgender* and is used as a complement to transgender. It is a word used to describe those individuals whose experience with gender matched their biological sex at birth. The prefix *cis-* means "on the side of" in Latin while *trans-* means "on the other side of." Although most people in our culture are cisgender, using the term allows us to acknowledge that there are those individuals who differ from the majority population.

Recently, there has been resurgence in the use of the word *queer* even though the term had negative and derogatory connotations decades ago. Queer is becoming an umbrella term for those individuals who do not fall under the societal categories of LGBT or the gender binary of male and female. In some ways, this term is becoming an inclusive and fluid label for the broader LGBTQ community. This is especially true for those who do not seem to fit within the normative categories of sexual identity in culture. The term also unites the LGBTQ community by what they have in common rather than using labels that highlight their differences. I have a hunch that in the coming years "queer community" may replace the phrase "LGBTQ community".

Another term that needs to be defined is *intersex*. Once called *hermaphrodites*, intersex people are genetically both male and female. Most intersex individuals have both male and female genitalia, as well as both sets of sex chromosomes. This is a very rare condition. Often, parents and doctors of intersex individuals decide what gender the child will be raised with, even though the person may decide to change their gender later in life. Also, intersex individuals can be attracted to either sex, be bisexual, or sometimes are asexual.

As with transgender individuals, it is beneficial to know what pronoun to use with intersex individuals, as well as catering to their needs by using gender-neutral activities that will create acceptance and a community of belonging. A friend of mine who is intersex shared how he had been kicked out of a church because he was using the female bathroom. Yet, when he used the men's bathroom, he would often get odd looks and comments. The churches he had been part of never asked him how they could help him feel accepted in the church or how they might cater to his needs as an intersex individual.

Although I have been using the term *LGBTQ community*, there are other words that are sometimes incorporated into this acronym. Some would expand the acronym to *LGBTQQQIAP community*. In addition to the LGBTQ terms previously discussed, it includes those who are *questioning* (their sexuality), *intersex* (defined above), *asexual* (those who have little or no sexual desire and attraction), and *pansexual* (those attracted to any gender or biological sex). It is a bit confusing to have such a large acronym, but the point is to be as inclusive and representative as possible. People identify themselves in numerous ways. Educating ourselves about their diverse and complex identities is one way we can reverse stereotypes and dehumanization. Of course, such an acronym will not cover every single person, and the more letters we add to it, the more obnoxious it can seem. Yet, it is all in hopes to represent humans. The above terminology is not meant to be labels or names. Instead, they are ways people identify themselves. In educating ourselves and learning how others identify themselves, we must continue to extend grace as we pursue hospitality.

CHAPTER THREE

The reason I believe adopting such language is a way to show love and hospitality is because we are called to serve others and meet people where they are. We recognize their felt needs instead of trying to fix what we perceive as their problems. Jesus met people's physical needs as a sign that He would meet their spiritual needs. He met people where they were, not where He thought they should be. It seems to me that behind all the labels, names, and identifiers, the LGBTQ community is, in their own way, seeking validation, identity, belonging, and acceptance. Most deeply, they are seeking what we all seek: love. Because we are called to put the needs and interests of other people before our own, as Philippians 2 reminds us for instance, we can serve others, learn their questions, needs, problems, and meet people where they are so we all can move forward into relationship with one another and with the God of Love.

Problematic Phrases

There is particular terminology that the broader Christian community uses about the LGBTQ community that often discredits Christians and hinders any productive dialogue with LGBTQ individuals. The LGBTQ community can see the Christian community coming from miles away simply because of a few terms that are only used by Christians. As you read, you may realize that you have used the terms or phrases I am telling you are offensive. I don't mean to make you feel guilty. We have all messed up, and it's okay. In my own journey, I have used terminology or labels to describe the LGBTQ community that I have later learned were offensive, unhelpful, or simply dismissive. My intentions were good, but my words revealed my ignorance.

I will begin with the phrase that is probably the most offensive: "Hate the sin; love the sinner." Many Christians frequently use this phrase when discussing the topic of homosexuality and think this is a loving and gracious phrase. We have been taught to think this. Unfortunately, it falls short. The LGBTQ community will discredit anything a Christian says or believes if he or she uses this phrase. To the LGBTQ individual, there is no differentiation between "the sin" and "the sinner" in that phrase. What they hear is, "Hate the sin; hate the sinner," or worse, simply, "I hate you." Again, for many individuals within the LGBTQ community, their identity is wrapped up into their sexual orientation, and they do not believe this orientation is sinful. When Christians, then, say they "hate the sin," many gays and lesbians feel as if their entire being is being attacked.[25]

To me, it seems using this phrase is a passive way out of difficult conversations. It is a close-ended statement that people use to dismiss other viewpoints. When used, it allows people to hide behind a phrase that isn't even biblical. Author and public speaker Tony Campolo argues that Christians should never utter this phrase, as it does not accurately reflect the teaching of the Bible. Instead, he purports that the Bible more clearly teaches, "Hate your own sin, and love everyone," as in Luke 6 when Jesus calls followers to deal with their own issues (the "plank in your eye") and love even their enemies.[26]

Another term Christians should no longer use to refer to an LGBTQ person is *homosexual*. At one point, I emailed a large group of gay friends to ask them if they find the term homosexual to be offensive. Many of them agreed that the term made sense and said they had even used it to describe themselves. However, almost all of them reminded me that the term had been hijacked by Christians and used in a derogatory way.

Currently, Christians seem to be the only ones using this term, and very few people in the LGBTQ community use the term to describe themselves. It is interesting to note that almost all heterosexual Christian scholars and writers who speak about homosexuality use the term *homosexual,* while almost no LGBTQ or progressive scholars use it.[27] When we use this term in conversation, we come across as ignorant, elementary, or that we apparently have no LGBTQ friendships. Instead of using this term, I recommend using *lesbian, gay, bisexual, or transgender* to describe those individuals within the broader community.

Other terms Christians are known to use that are not helpful in creating honest dialogue with the LGBTQ community are *choice, lifestyle, or struggle.* There is no doubt that there are Christians who believe gay individuals have chosen their orientation, though other Christians believe individuals do not choose their orientation, but rather discover it. Regardless of one's belief, these terms are belittling to those within the LGBTQ community. For many, it is not a choice, or a lifestyle, or even a struggle, but an aspect of their personality and identity.

Words have the power to encourage life as well as wither it. As the book of Proverbs reminds us, they have the power to bring life, to be as sweet as honey and to be a healing balm to the soul. At the same time, our words can bring death, be a poison, and wound the soul. This is apparent when we think of the countless suicides of gay youth due to bullying. Words have the power to affect people so much that they take their own lives. We must stand up against this, especially if we are Christians. Any bullying of gay youth, or any gay man or woman, should be immediately stopped. For Christians, calling other people "faggots," "fags," or flippantly saying certain things are "gay" or "queer" is grossly antithetical to Christian living. Because Christians are commanded to say only words of love and use those words to edify others (see Eph. 4:29), such negative language directed toward the LGBTQ community is unacceptable. All those in ministry, especially those in youth ministry where this terminology is often present, should combat this type of derogatory language. It has absolutely no place within the Christian community or the Christian's vernacular.

I would be remiss if I didn't remind us of the power of our words as we move forward in difficult conversations. I have had countless conversations about homosexuality and the Church. These dialogues can bring up deep passion, raise tempers, and even escalate into arguments. I have often been reminded of Proverbs 15:1 that says, "A gentle answer turns away wrath, but a harsh word stirs up anger." As we move forward,

CHAPTER THREE

I hope that we would embody this verse—that as we gently share our answers, our words would never stir up anger but be full of grace. It is one of the most hospitable acts we can do.

Gay and Christian

In conclusion, I want to address what is, for many, the most difficult topic to discuss and understand. In certain Christian circles, it is thought to be impossible to be both gay and Christian. For those who believe this, being gay is either a choice or a sinful action and being a Christian yet choosing to be gay or act in a sinful way is impossible. Yet, I propose that the term "gay Christian" should not be an oxymoron for heterosexual Christians. Too often, for many heterosexuals, the term "gay" immediately is defined by what happens in the bedroom behind closed doors. However, the term should be defined not by sexual actions but by attraction, just as "heterosexual" means someone attracted to the opposite sex. If "gay" means one who is attracted to the same sex and "Christian" means one who follows Jesus Christ as Lord, then these words are not mutually exclusive. Other adjectives put before "Christian" *would* make an oxymoron—"hateful Christian" or "judgmental Christian" might be two good examples. One who is sexually attracted to someone of the same sex and also professes Jesus Christ as Lord can rightly call him or herself a gay Christian.

I happen to have a good friend who is one of the most knowledgeable Christians I know. I learn about

God from his actions and life. He is a pastor who cares deeply for his congregation. His preaching is amazing. He loves the Lord, and I know that the Holy Spirit dwells within him. He loves hymns, knows Scripture, and is humble, kind, loving, patient, gracious, and gentle. He loves communion and was baptized and confirmed into the Church. He is also gay. He also has high standards for his sexual actions. Due to his faith in God, he is not sexually promiscuous, but believes in monogamy and that he should be holy in the way he acts. He believes in a monogamous marriage between two people, which can include two people of the same sex. To dismiss him as not being a true Christian or deny the truth of his sexual identity is unfair and wrong.

Rather than debating whether or not gays and lesbians can be Christian, it might be more appropriate to question whether putting any adjective before the word *Christian* is a good idea. If Christ is truly our all in all, is it beneficial to modify the term with an adjective? Perhaps the term *Christian* functions better by itself. When both heterosexual and gay Christians live out their call to be Christ-like, orientation can often become a secondary matter. For the Christian, holiness is an important life goal regardless of orientation. Both gay and heterosexual Christians pursue holiness in all areas of their lives, because Jesus calls each of His followers to be holy as God is holy.

Adjectives and labels have a profound effect on shaping our identity and our view of others. In many church communities, I have been reminded that I am a sinner, that I am unholy, unclean, or a filthy rag before

God. I've found that the more I am told I am a sinner, the more easily I believe it. The more easily I believe it, the more easily it is for me to live out that identity. I think to myself, "Since I am a sinner, I guess I will just sin. I doubt I'll ever stop sinning, because I'm a sinner." This belief also shapes how we view other Christians. We see them as sinners, unholy, or unclean, and so we exclude, demean, or fear them.

In the New Testament, there are over 40 times where the words "sinner" or "sinners" appear. Yet, none of these refer to someone who has come to a saving faith in the Lord Jesus. **Never is a person with saving faith in Jesus Christ called a sinner.** A Christian is never labeled a "sinner" in the Bible. This is radically Good News that can radically affect our lives and identity.

The Good News is that Jesus lived a perfectly sinless life and died a horrible death. Yet, because of Jesus' life, death, and resurrection, Christ's sinless, holy, and perfect life has been transferred to us. Now, God views us as if we lived the sinless and holy life that Jesus lived.[28] Christ took the punishment that we so deserved. Christ's resurrection signifies that we will also be raised to new life. Therefore, we are no longer sinners. Instead, we are beloved children of the Most High God. **We are saints—saints who happen to sin once in a while.**

Yes, my sexual orientation is an aspect of my identity, just as being a pastor, son, brother, husband, and artist are aspects of my identity. For those in the LGBTQ community, their orientation is an aspect of their identity, perhaps one they see as defining them more profoundly than many heterosexuals do. But such aspects, nor our sin, can never trump our identity as saints. Christ defines our identity. More than our gender, orientation, race, or class, our Christian identity is stronger than any other identifier. I wonder if we need to do a better job preaching the truth of our identity as saints to one another rather than preaching that we are sinners. Wouldn't it be great news to hear sermons that proclaim what you do does not define your identity, but rather God defines your identity? I wonder if our LGBTQ brothers and sisters would be encouraged to hear us say that in Christ they too are fully loved, fully cherished, and fully known children of the Most High God.

4

CHAPTER FOUR

how do we read the six main passages?

What does the Bible say about homosexuality? How should I read it?" I asked these questions for years, and I assume I am not the only one. I was definitely taught one way to read the Bible concerning the definition and treatment of homosexuality. As I continued to meet different people with different experiences, however, I also met people with different theological conclusions. Some reflected my own thoughts and some were starkly opposed. Some were gracious as they explained their reasons for reading Scripture a particular way, while the rest treated me as if I were stupid to believe as I did.

As time went on, I became more and more confused about what the Bible actually said about homosexuality. From what I was reading and hearing, some people believed that the Bible said homosexuality was sinful, yet others seemed to profess that the Bible was not speaking of homosexuality as we know it today in our culture. When I decided to spend more than one year writing my seminary thesis on the six main Bible passages regarding homosexuality, I read traditional scholars and understood and even agreed with how they came to their interpretation. However, when I read more progressive scholars, I found myself agreeing with their interpretation and conclusions. So which side was right?

In my reading, it was clear there were two sides to the debate concerning homosexuality. There is the conservative or traditional side, and there are those who land on the progressive or revisionist side. In both groups are strong and committed Christians, scholars and professors, pastors and preachers, lay leaders and average congregants. Some are incredibly gracious in their approach, while others are passionately judgmental with their treatment of the other side. However, both sides have done their homework, respect the Bible, and have countless arguments that undergird their interpretations.

Before we feel the urge to dismiss certain scholars or theological opinions that differ from our own, we need to be reminded of the humanity of both sides. I have met many conservatives who are not bigots full of hatred. I also know many progressives who are not crazy liberals believing nothing is sinful. We have demonized one another in our debates, but now we need to humanize each other. We are not enemies, but are part of the family of God as sisters and brothers in Christ, doing our best to read and meditate upon God's Word and live lives worthy of the calling God has given us.

In some conversations I have had with people over this topic, it seemed they came to their biblical beliefs through a light reading of the text. "Well, the Bible says homosexuality is sin. It's right there in black and white, so that's what I believe." Others simply said, "Because Jesus said nothing about homosexuality, I'm fine with it and don't believe it is a sin." It also seemed to me that neither side wanted to learn, let alone listen to how the other side came to their conclusions. Both of these approaches, I felt, diminish the beauty of Scripture and the interpretation process. Both are dismissive. As Christians who uphold the Bible as the Word of God, we must treat it with more respect and honor than that.

However, one of the best ways for us to have fruitful dialogue and remain united is to learn both sides of the debate. This not only helps in our own understanding of the Bible, but also allows us to have faithful and graceful conversations with people whose views differ from our own.

For example, there are a few biblical texts that have been interpreted to teach that women should not be preachers or pastors. At the same time, there are numerous biblical texts that promote women in all fields of leadership within the Church. The same could be said about opposing interpretations of the biblical passages pertaining to adult or infant baptism. Learning both sides of this debate can do numerous things. It can help us understand our own theological viewpoints better and deeper. It can help us understand the other side's view and allow us to dialogue with them. And it can even change our understanding as we realize God is leading us in a different way. When we learn both sides of the debate, we become better theologians, more understanding and gracious, and better partners for dialogue.

Building friendships with LGBTQ individuals and gaining a thorough understanding of both sides of the theological interpretations of homosexuality has forced numerous pastors and God-fearing men and women I know to rethink their former conclusions and even change their views. I also know of parents of LGBTQ individuals who have changed their opinion on this topic after years of conversations with their gay or lesbian child. When you personally know someone who is gay or lesbian, it changes the way you view this debate.

My goal is not to convince anyone that certain theological beliefs, especially if they are traditional, are wrong. We all need to be reminded that our interpretations affect people, and that the better versed we are in interpretational differences, the better our dialogue and relationships can be. My aim in this chapter is to offer help in understanding both sides of the debate. Therefore, this chapter will have a lot of information. Much of this comes from my own thesis on the six main biblical passages pertaining to homosexuality.[29] However, this is only an overview and starting point. Through it all, my hope is that you will consult with God, other scholars, and countless other resources, as you prayerfully discern where you may eventually land.

CHAPTER FOUR

Is Sodom and Gomorrah about Homosexuality or Inhospitality?

Let's begin with quite possibly the most famous Bible story that references homosexuality—the story of Sodom and Gomorrah in Genesis 19. The story follows Lot, who invites two visiting angels to stay at his house in Sodom. Upon arriving at Lot's home, men from the city of Sodom surround the house, boldly urging Lot to bring the visitors outside so the men of Sodom might get to "know" them (some translations say "have sex with" them). Instead, Lot offers his two virgin daughters to the mob of men. However, the men reject the daughters and become increasingly violent. As the story continues, the visiting angels then strike the mob of men with blindness. Later in the well-known passage, God destroys both Sodom and Gomorrah as Lot and his family are fleeing the city.

Many people argue that both cities were destroyed because of the rampant homosexuality within them. But is this story about homosexuality? Some Christians think it definitely is, while others think it has nothing to do with it. For those who are more traditional, this passage reveals the depravity of humanity, that men would have sex with other men, requiring God's judgment. Yet, for those who are more progressive, this text is not about homosexuality, but rather inhospitality, gang rape, greed, indifference to the poor, and general wickedness.

my own view originally.

I can see this but as a different possible explanation

64

The Traditional Stance on Sodom and Gomorrah

Many traditional readings focus on the Hebrew word, *yadha*, which is translated, "to know" or "to have sex with" in Genesis 19:5: "Where are the men who came to you tonight? Bring them out so we may *know* them." The word, which appears 956 times throughout the Old Testament, is often translated "to know," "to get acquainted with," or "to get familiar with."[30] However, approximately 10 to 16 times throughout the Old Testament, in Genesis in particular, the word *yadha* denotes sexual intercourse.[31] In this passage, then, it is argued that "to know" really should be translated "to have sex with."

Another reason it is assumed the men of Sodom had intentions to sexually assault Lot's visitors and not simply get "acquainted with" them was the fact that Lot offered his two virgin daughters, "who have not known a man," to the mob in lieu of the visitors. The context implies that he was offering them to be sexually used instead.[32] This, and the fact that the men's violence increased after Lot offered his daughters, suggests to traditional scholars that the sin of Sodom was not merely inhospitality or attempted rape of a visitor, but an attempted same-sex rape of male visitors, which ultimately reveals the utter depravity of humanity.[33] Such acts as these went against God's plan for humanity and God's intentions for sex, and therefore needed to be judged and repented of.[34]

The Progressive Stance on Sodom and Gomorrah

Progressive scholars argue that the story of Sodom and Gomorrah is really about inhospitality, greed, injustice, mistreatment of foreigners, excess of wealth, and general wickedness. In progressive interpretations, the men of Sodom intended to gang rape these men as a sign of power rather than sexual attraction. Lot protected them as his guests, for hospitality toward strangers was an extremely important custom in that culture. It was more appropriate to protect the male visitors in their house than women, which is why Lot offered his daughters to the mob instead. If the men of Sodom were gay and acting on same-sex desires, Lot would not have offered the women for them to abuse.[35]

Progressives also point out that among the numerous other references to Sodom throughout the Bible,[36] none of them reference homosexuality, while all of them affirm that the city was destroyed because of inhospitality. All the verses refer to injustice, indifference to the poor, greed, or general wickedness. The sins of Sodom are most thoroughly described in Ezekiel 16:49-50, which says, "…this was the guilt of your sister Sodom: she and her daughters had pride, excess of food, and prosperous ease, but did not aid the poor and needy. They were haughty and did detestable things before me." Even Jesus' comments on Sodom in Luke 10:12 and Matthew 10:15 refer to the city's refusal of hospitality to travelers.[37]

A parallel passage to Genesis 19 can be found in Judges 19. In this story, a Levite is traveling with his concubine and servant to Gibeah. After stopping in Gibeah's town square for the night, they meet an old man originally from the country of Ephraim who insists that they not stay in the town square, invites them home with him, and provides foot-washing, food, and drink. During this time, men of the city surround the house and demand that the old man give them the traveling Levite so that they may "know" him or "have sex with him." Instead, the man sends out his concubine, who is repeatedly raped throughout the night and killed. The town is later destroyed for its wickedness. The story, like Genesis 19, highlights a mob group of people who sought to humiliate the traveler by same-sex rape, and then proceeded to gang rape a young woman to death. Both texts, it is argued, are not about same-sex desire, but violence, abuse, and inhospitality.

The temptation is to look only at the sexual act found in this passage and make an easy correlation between homosexuality and God's condemnation. Yet, this story is not about the sexual act alone, but about the countless behaviors comprising such a heinous, inhospitable act. For many, then, Genesis 19 does not denounce homosexuality, but injustice, greed, inhospitality, gang rape, and indifference to the poor. With this understanding, this text can be powerfully applicable to many Christians in our current American culture, more than we might care to think.

CHAPTER FOUR

Leviticus Says Homosexuality is an Abomination?

Any time I have been challenged to read the Bible from beginning to end, I have often given up right around the Book of Leviticus. If I do make it through, I usually get stuck right around 1 or 2 Chronicles. They are brutal. Leviticus has never been one of my favorite books, and my guess is it probably isn't a favorite of many others, either. I don't know of many pastors who have preached through Leviticus, or churches that hope it shows up in the lectionary more regularly. Leviticus is full of laws and rules. At a most basic level, we know it is the book that condemns tattoos, wearing mixed fibers, planting two seeds in one garden, and calls homosexuality an abomination punishable by death.

There are two verses in the Book of Leviticus that are quite bold in their prohibition against same-sex intercourse. Leviticus 18:22 says, "Do not lie with a man as one lies with a woman; that is detestable," while 20:13 commands, "If a man lies with a man as one lies with a woman, both of them have done what is detestable. They must be put to death; their blood will be on their own heads." Both of these verses are found in what is known in Leviticus as the Holiness Code.

The Traditional Stance on Leviticus

At the center of the Holiness Code is the command to the Israelites in Leviticus 19:2: "Be holy, for I the

LORD your God am holy." God requires the covenant people to be holy and abstain from certain practices, so as to distinguish the Israelites from other nations. Neighboring nations and cultures were practicing homosexuality and allowed bestiality and other sexual practices addressed in Leviticus 20 and 21. Numerous prohibitions appear in these chapters, including eating certain meat, incest, bestiality, stealing, lying, cheating, shaving, tattoos, wearing clothes made from two different fabrics, and trimming one's forelocks, among others.[38] The death penalty is the punishment not only for same-sex behavior, but also for sacrificing children, adultery, incest, sleeping with in-laws, bestiality, and for priest's daughters who become prostitutes.

In Leviticus, same-sex intercourse is described as "detestable," or an "abomination," some translations say. The Hebrew word used here is *toevah*, which appears throughout Leviticus and is also used in the book of Deuteronomy. *Toevah* refers to an act that is considered abhorrent or repugnant, such as idolatry or inappropriate worship of God.[39] Many scholars and Christians believe that homosexuality is not what God originally designed and intended for humanity. It is detestable or an abomination, because it goes against God's creation of humanity as male and female. Men were not created to have natural sex with men, while the same is true for women with women. Because of this, homosexuality is a form of idolatry or inappropriate worship.

Unlike other Levitical commands that are no longer upheld, commands against homosexuality are upheld as a part of the broader Old Testament narrative and also upheld in the New Testament. Because the language used in Leviticus is absolute and is grouped with other sexual practices that are still prohibited today, such as incest, bestiality, and child sacrifice, many Christians maintain homosexuality must be condemned.

The Progressive Stance on Leviticus

Scholars who argue the progressive stance do not reject the idea that same-sex intercourse is considered a sin in these particular texts in the Levitical law. Many Christians agree that Leviticus condemns same-sex intercourse for that particular time and culture, but question how or whether these verses apply to modern culture. For progressive individuals, such questioning does not dismiss or diminish Scripture, but reasons that our application of these passages must be shaped by an understanding of the contemporary culture and framework in which Leviticus was written. Today, in a different time and culture, such restrictions may not be applicable, just as we no longer follow certain laws that used to exist in our own nation.

Some people have asked why we uphold the prohibitions in Leviticus 18:22 and 20:13 so sternly, yet reject the death penalty they prescribe, as well as other prohibitions found in the same passage. If the punishment is no longer applied to the offense, these scholars ask, could it be that the offense is no longer offensive? This is quite a jump for many of us. As we know, changes have occurred in Christian interpretations of Scripture. There are numerous practices that the

Bible permits, such as polygamy, concubinage, or levirate marriage, which we currently refuse to accept. Yet, there are other actions the Bible condemns that have been reconsidered on the basis of what we know in our current culture, such as divorce and remarriage.[40]

Progressive Christians make the point that the term *toevah*, acts considered "detestable" or "abominable," also refers to that which is "unclean" or "impure." Other translations are "dirtiness" or "taboo."[41] Another Hebrew word that could have been used to describe same-sex intercourse is *zimah*. This term often denotes something that is an injustice, morally wrong, or a sin. Leviticus, though, does not call same-sex intercourse *zimah*, but *toevah*. Therefore, many people conclude that homosexuality was something that was unclean or dirty, not something that was so sinful or morally wrong that it deserved death or mistreatment.

The progressive conclusion is that there were different categories of sin. Certain actions were wrong or evil, while other actions—such as having sex with a menstruating woman, eating pork, or wearing clothing of the opposite sex (not all at the same time, of course)—were considered unclean. Unclean acts would separate people from the Temple, or the place of worship, until they had gone through the certain practices that would make them clean again. Also, while some types of unclean acts are conscious personal or physical acts, a person could also be considered unclean simply from contact with certain physical objects or actions.

Some argue that homosexuality made one unclean in the same way that touching an unclean animal or

bird is a *toevah*.[42] And, because we have done away
with such prohibitions, some Christians believe it is
fair to assume we need to do the same with the Levitical prohibition against same-sex acts. Progressive
Christians argue that understanding the historical and
cultural context exposes the traditional interpretations of the same-sex laws as misguided and harmful
to Christians who are a part of the LGBTQ community.
While agreeing that in the Levitical context same-sex
intercourse is considered sin, they question whether
a sexual ethic for today can be derived from such a
difficult and different context. They wonder if homosexuality can truly be condemned in the harsh way our
Bibles are translated, and whether these prohibitions
were solely for a different time and place.

Jesus and the Law

As we can see, the book of Leviticus is full of laws,
and the debate around homosexuality stems from
how to interpret the Law. My own difficulty in studying these passages is that I am not a Hebrew scholar,
nor am I completely versed in Jewish culture. Both
of these things would add to this discussion. There
is no doubt that the Bible we read and study is complicated and perplexing. Yet, this is the beauty of the
Bible. **We should not run from texts we do not fully
understand, and we should not use texts as a weapon,
either.** Our job is to be faithful.

Jesus was always picked on for either following or
not following the Law. There were times when people

thought He was interpreting it wrongly or simply disregarding it completely. Yet, Christ came to fulfill the Law, redeem the Law, and embody the Law. Jesus also never demanded that we followed every iota of the Law before we could follow Him. In a time when the normal practice was to clean oneself up before being able to approach the invisible God, Jesus, the visible God, came to people as they were. Jesus never used texts to divide and condemn sin but instead used them to bring life, proclaim Good News to the poor, bring freedom to the prisoners, heal the blind and sick, set the oppressed free, and proclaim the year of the Lord's favor. My hope is that we can do the same.

Does Romans 1 Condemn Homosexuality or Idolatry?

The Book of Romans contains one of the most crucial texts in the debate concerning homosexuality. I have heard people argue that this passage is very clear in its condemnation of homosexuality. Other people believe Paul is using homosexuality as an interpretative example and is condemning a particular sexual cultural practice. So, which is it? This passage is more difficult to dismiss than the Old Testament passages, and, for many progressives, it is the hardest to overturn. My hope is to simply highlight a few aspects of each view as a starting point for digging into these passages.

A conversation with one of my closest friends, who happens to be gay, opened my eyes to the importance of studying Scripture in community and learning from a diverse group of people. Keith and I had been friends for close to six years. We had performed as actors at a couple of the same theatres, had a similar group of friends, and had been roommates twice during our friendship. Until studying Romans 1 for my thesis, I read this text simply and literally. Because the English translation of my Bible spoke out against homosexuality, I believed it. Then, in my studies, I came across a scholar who, although still traditional in his understanding of homosexuality, was the most gracious conservative scholar I had read. He highlighted points I had never thought of and brought me to a deeper understanding of the text.

Excited about these new insights, I brought them up in conversation with Keith while spending time at his apartment. I presented what I had learned and how my opinion had changed. I discussed how this scholar had shown me that homosexuality was not what God intended, but that I did not have the place to judge. Asking my friend what he thought, he responded that as a gay man that interpretation could not work for him and explained why it actually hurt him. The interpretation, whether I said it or not, made him feel as if he was less than human. In his mind, such a belief said to him that God didn't design him the way he was, or that in God's eyes Keith wasn't a beautiful, human fully loved by God.

We continued in conversation for a while, going back and forth in our debate, never trying to convince one another but discussing how and why certain interpretations could and could not work. I realized after that conversation that I still needed to study and discern where God was leading me, as well as realize that I could not read only one side of the debate to get a fair representation of viewpoints.

What struck me the most was the realization that our deep friendship was what mattered most. The only reason we could have such an honest and open conversation was the fact that we had been friends for six years. If we had tried to have a similar conversation the moment I found out Keith was gay or even within the first year of our friendship, I am not sure our friendship would have lasted. At that point, defending our theological beliefs might have been more important to us than our friendship. After six long years as friends and roommates, however, our relationship mattered much more than defending our theological beliefs.

The lesson I have learned, which I hope comes across throughout this book, is that relationships matter. Learning these passages on their own does not help unless we are in relationship with LGBTQ individuals and people who have different opinions than our own. **When we anchor our relationships in the fact that each of us are God's beloved children, instead of trying to prove our theological convictions, our debates become discussions and our friendships will hold strong.** My relationship with Keith has strengthened and deepened how I view these passages, especially Romans 1, and I believe Keith's relationship with me has strengthened and deepened how he views Scripture, too. Keith and I know that we are brothers, both sons of the Most High God, and that matters more to us than our opinions about particular passages within the Bible.

Romans 1 from a Traditional Stance

Paul begins his letter by greeting the Roman Christians and expressing his own desire to visit the city. In one of my favorite verses, and one I struggle to live out if I'm honest, Paul declares that he is "not ashamed of the Gospel because it is the power of God that brings salvation to everyone who believes" (Romans 1:16). He then reminds them that God's displeasure is being revealed, because people have known God but refused to treat God as such. People have worshipped and served created things rather than worshipping and serving the Creator. Homosexuality is one result of this idolatry, among many other destructive attitudes and behaviors. This text still reminds us of our own struggle to resist giving our utmost to created things, prioritizing them before all else, rather than giving our utmost to Christ, our King and Lord.

For many traditional believers, Paul uses homosexuality in this passage as the prime example of humanity's perversion and overt sinfulness. Because Paul is discussing idolatry, the implication is that homosexuality is a manifestation of this false worship—the worship of desires and passion above God. God's judgment against such idolatry is a passive "giving them over" to sinful desires. God allows humanity the freedom to act as they wish and pursue their own passions, which in this case is same-sex intercourse.[43]

Other Christians point out Paul's implication that homosexuality is also a result of suppressing God's truth. Scripture, anatomy, and sexual norms affirm that heterosexuality is natural human sexuality.

Homosexuality perverts natural sex by exchanging the desire for the opposite sex for the same sex, and is a self-degrading behavior that dishonors one's own body.[44]

However, many Christians believe that simply using Romans 1 as a blanket condemnation of gays and lesbians, or outside the context of Romans 1-3, does a disservice to the text and Paul's argument. Romans 2:1 is a clear reminder that all have done wrong against God, are guilty of worshipping the created things, and do not have the right to judge. It says, "You, therefore, have no excuse, you who pass judgment on someone else, for at whatever point you judge another, you are condemning yourself, because you who pass judgment do the same things." Christians, even those who believe that homosexuality is sinful, have no right to condemn any gay or lesbian person any more than they would condemn the sin in their own lives. At the same time, even if someone is a progressive or LGBTQ Christian, he or she does not have a right to judge more conservative Christians.

Many of those who interpret Romans 1 in a more conservative light are not blatant bigots or full of hatred. I have found many conservatives to be incredibly gracious. Although the interpretation comes across as black and white, many Christians are not dismissive of LGBTQ people or inherently without compassion.

Romans 1: What About the Other Side?

How can other Christians read this passage in Romans 1 and say with any sort of confidence that Paul is not condemning homosexuality as sinful? In order to answer that question, many progressive Christians think we must have a better understanding of Greek culture and the practice of pederasty. In Greek culture, pederasty was the sexual practice of an adult male who had sexual relations with a young boy, usually an adolescent close to the time of puberty. In a culture that viewed beauty purely in a physical sense and often held young males up as the key symbol for male eroticism,[45] pederasty was a widely acceptable practice. This is very different than our current culture that objectifies women as the sexual ideal.

Men who practiced pederasty were not necessarily gay. Most of the time, these men were married to women and participated in such relationships on the side. At times, these relationships were abusive or full of inequality. Many such relationships were non-committal, as the older male went from one attractive boy to the next.[46] Because the culture at the time was hierarchical and slave-based, many young slaves were forced into sexual encounters with older men because of their lower status.[47] With this being the context in which the Romans lived, progressives believe Paul is speaking against abusive male pederastic relationships rather than homosexuality as it is known in our current culture.

Others progressives admit that Paul is condemning homosexuality, inequality, or pederasty in his cultural context, but point out that his broader argument is idolatry and the unrighteousness of the Gentiles and the Jews. Therefore, some Christians believe, Paul is not making an ethical argument on sexuality, but instead he is making a theological argument that all of humanity, both Jews and Gentiles, are guilty of worshipping the created rather than the Creator.[48] Because Paul quickly drops the subject of homosexuality in this passage, many people believe it is not the main substance of Paul's argument. Instead, these chapters are a presentation of the Gospel. Paul's thesis is found in verse 16, that he is not ashamed of the Gospel, which is the power of God for the salvation of all people.

A lot of this information was brand new to me as I started researching and learning about these passages and cultural practices. I did not know how to pronounce the word "pederasty," let alone know what it was or how it worked in Greek culture. Learning about it has been incredibly interesting, especially because of my studies in Greek drama during my undergraduate studies. It was almost as if Paul was writing to a bunch of Christians living in Las Vegas or Amsterdam where the cultural practices of those cities seeped into daily Christian life and hindered their distinctiveness.

As mentioned previously, this passage speaks of women and men exchanging what was *natural* for what was *unnatural* in relation to homosexuality. Romans 1:26-27 reads, "Even their women exchanged natural sexual relations for unnatural ones. In the same way the men also abandoned *natural* relations with women..." For progressive Christians, looking at the particular Greek words Paul uses is helpful in the discussion. Paul uses the two words *physin* and *para physin*, which mean "natural" and "unnatural" or "against nature." However, they argue, the term *physin* or "natural" does not necessarily mean universal nature or actions. The word also means that which is ordinary, characteristic, expected, and even regular for a particular group or person.[49]

The term *para physin*, on the other hand, means "against nature" or "contrary to nature." Being "contrary to nature" does not mean opposition to the natural laws of the universe, but rather contrary to what is normal. Although *para* can mean "against," it can also mean "beside," "more than," "beyond," or "over and above." The Greek word is even used in reference to God later in the Book of Romans as God acts in an unnatural way by incorporating the Gentiles into the body of believers. A contemporary example of such a definition would be someone who does not like singing, but contrary to his or her nature decides to enter a karaoke contest.

This uncharacteristic behavior is why the text speaks of men and women who went from what was natural (sex acts with the opposite sex) to what was contrary to their nature (sex acts with the same sex). Because of this, progressives argue, those who participated in same-sex acts were not wrong, going against God, or even contrary to creation. Instead, such sex acts were not the ones these people usually performed.[50] The people in this text, as is often assumed, were not gay or lesbian individuals, but rather heterosexuals that went against what was characteristic of them. Idolatry caused them to lust with desire and act in atypical ways.

A seminal book on this text comes from James V. Brownson, New Testament Professor at Western Theological Seminary. *Bible, Gender, Sexuality: Reframing the Church's Debate on Same-Sex Relationships* gives a thorough and clear survey of this topic. He maintains that Paul is arguing that sinfulness, which includes all of humanity, is an inward problem.[51] Although same-sex behavior is spoken in negative terms in Romans 1, Paul is arguing that the uncontrollable excess of sexual desire is what leads to sin. Yet, Brownson questions whether all gay relationships today are based off of uncontrollable sexual desire instead of mutual love.[52]

Brownson echoes the voices above that explain Paul's use of the word "natural" and "unnatural" as being those that are uncharacteristic. He contends, though, that there were three aspects of "nature" that we must understand today: an individual disposition, social order, and procreation. The excessive sexual behavior that is described in Romans 1 is "unnatural" because it violated the personal disposition of those involved because it was the result of excessive lust and desire. It went against what was customary and natural for a person at the time.[53]

The second understanding of "nature" that Brownson explains involves the social structure and gender roles that were prevalent in the culture. The behaviors Paul describes confused and distorted the societal gender roles at the time, which although different than our own today, were considered normal and natural.[54]

Finally, Paul describes the behaviors as unnatural because they went against the procreative aspects of sex. Any form of sexual behavior that did not end in procreation was considered "unnatural." This was the interpretation of this passage for the first 300 years of the church and explains why lesbianism is mentioned.[55]

Brownson's book is an important read and he has a voice we must listen to as we continue to discern whether the Bible speaks of same-sex relationships as we know them today. His book gives a great framework for people who are hoping to learn more and even reconsider the interpretations about sexuality found within the Bible. He forces his reader to wonder whether the Bible's condemnation of same-sex relationships in an ancient culture can be applied to the contemporary relationships we see today. Although he does not openly answer that question, he does propose that we need to discern more clearly how best to respond to the LGBTQ community and loving and consensual same-sex relationships today.

How Do You Even Pronounce the Greek Words for Homosexuality?

The final two passages I'll discuss are 1 Corinthians 6:9 and 1 Timothy 1:10. This is the final stretch and might seem like a short foreign language course because we are looking at a couple Greek words that are very difficult to translate into English. Both passages are lists that describe certain behaviors as unacceptable for Christians. Writing to the church in

Corinth, a city where lawlessness was rampant among Christ followers, Paul lists examples of wicked behavior, including the sexually immoral, idolaters, adulterers, "male prostitutes," and "homosexual offenders," among others. 1 Timothy, a letter of encouragement and instruction to a young pastor, describes people who are rebels, ungodly, and sinful. Paul lists murderers, adulterers, and "perverts" or "homosexuals" as such examples.

These two passages have caused a lot of confusion and spurred a lot of scholarly work. Most of it hinges on the translations of two Greek words: *arsenokoites* and *malakos*. Reading these words in English can often confuse the reader as they are translated as "homosexual," "pervert," or "male prostitutes." The two words are incredibly rare and the meanings of both are often debated. For some, the translations confirm that homosexuality is listed as a sin, while for other people the translation reveals that homosexuality is not being referenced at all.

I find it interesting how dehumanizing our English translations of these words can be. We translate them as "pervert," which often connotes child molesters. They are also translated "prostitute," which is an illegal, shunned practice in our culture. Therefore, when we use the word to mean something in relation to homosexuality, we inevitably mean some action that is illegal or perverted. It seems to me that these words are not interchangeable in the English language. It is no wonder that many heterosexuals, then, can come to the utterly dehumanizing conclusions that gay people are molesters or sexually devious.

Let's begin with the term *arsenokoitai*, which is not found in any other Greek text earlier than 1 Corinthians.[56] It is a word made up from two words "male" (*arsen*) and "bed" or "lying" (*koite*). From this comes the basic translations of "men who lie with men," or "men who have sex with other men." It is often assumed that *arsenokoitai* refers to the male who takes the more active role in male-to-male intercourse, especially since it follows the passive *malakos.* However, some people find this method of translating a compound word problematic, as it is not how we usually come to define such words.[57] For instance, people use the words "understand," "butterfly," or "brainwash" to illustrate how compound words are not always defined as the combination of two words.

What is the context of those sins in which this word is listed? It would make sense that homosexuality would be in a list of other sins such as adultery, prostitution, or illicit sex. However, in 1 Corinthians, the list focuses on economic injustices and exploitations. Remembering the common practice of pederasty, many people believe that this word references some sort of exploitative sexual act.[58]

Is it possible that how we translate this word into English is insufficient? At times, I think so. Could it be that we might never know what Paul truly meant by this word? I think it is quite possible. Paul is believed to have invented this word. In the same way, William Shakespeare created words during his life that we might never fully understand. Yet, we do not debate the meanings of particular words from Shakespeare to such a degree. This is the difficulty of the Bible, as it is

Handwritten margin notes:

1 Cor. 6:9-10 Strongs- 733 or 3120 Arsenokoitai - Malakos (Resp.) homosexual or affimints (Resp) im: middle of other sexual ideas not economic injustic or exploitations.

a translated book. We must, though, continue to treat it with respect and study it with diligence.

The word *malakos* literally means "soft," but has often been translated as "effeminate." It can refer to the softness of clothing or fabric, the tenderness of food, or the gentleness of words. It is only used two other times in the New Testament (Matthew 11:8 and Luke 7:25), and a handful of times in the Old Testament (Proverbs 15:15, 26:22 and Job 41:3).[59] Some believe that this word is slang and can describe men, such as young boys in a pederastic relationship, as "soft" or "effeminate."[60] Because *malakos* is used in reference to *arsenokoites* in 1 Corinthians, it is often believed the translation "male prostitute" is correct.

Progressive individuals note that *malakos* has been translated in numerous ways over the last 50 years. At times it was "effeminate," then eventually became "catamite," "male prostitute," and even "homosexual perversion."[61] These different English translations all mean very different things, adding confusion to the actual meaning of the word. The term "soft" can also mean laziness, lack of courage, or simply effeminate. Women, for instance, were often considered weak, vulnerable, or tender, meaning they were *malakos*. Additionally, men who were lazy, refused to do manual labor, cowards, or even were living in luxury could be called "effeminate."[62]

In our own culture, being effeminate can be looked down upon as a way to express one's gender. But using a word from Scripture to label it sinful does not seem right. If we use the word "effeminate" as another way to describe someone who is gay, we have dehumanized and judged. There are stereotypes that gay men are effeminate, but this is not always the case, and to think that is simply wrong. Similarly, a woman who happens to be more masculine, or "butch," does not mean she is a lesbian. It is unfair for us to judge other people and their sexual orientation by the way they express their gender. Jesus looked to people's hearts, their inner motivations and longings. It is time we lay down our opinions and judgments of people's outward expression and learn their inner character and heart.

For progressive scholars and Christians, the discussion of homosexuality in this passage is closely tied to the Greco-Roman society where pederasty and male prostitution were normative sexual behaviors.[63] These relationships were not what we would currently label as loving same-sex relationships. Therefore, coming to decisions about modern day same-sex relationships from this passage alone, according to progressives, is incorrect.

Concluding Our Oscillation

I once saw a gentleman holding a sign with the words, "Here's what Jesus said about homosexuality:" written across the top. The rest of the poster was blank—and it's true. According to the Gospels, Jesus was entirely silent on the topic of homosexuality and spoke very little about sexuality.[64] Because of this, people come to the conclusion that Jesus would affirm homosexuality today. Others believe that Jesus was silent on the subject because He upheld the Jewish Old Testament teachings on sexuality.

As we can see, it is very easy to take the same passage of Scripture and come to different conclusions. People do it in regards to what Jesus does or does not say, and they do it using six passages of Scripture. As I mentioned earlier, I have oscillated in my own understanding of these texts. Scholars on both sides of the debate who have researched these passages have done a truly wonderful and faithful job. They have come at these texts through different lenses, experiences, and expertise.

There are Christians who believe the Bible is very clear in condemning homosexuality. Taken with church history and the Christian tradition, it is evident that homosexuality is not what God had intended for humanity. On the other side, there are Christians who conclude that the Bible does not speak to homosexuality as it exists in our current culture, but instead discusses same-sex practices that were culturally abusive, taboo, and exploitative. Brevity wins out in looking at these passages of Scripture. There is no doubt that scholars have spilt many pages of ink about these few verses. Where I have been too brief, please forgive, and where I have been challenging, please do more research.

Let me again say that my focus on these six major passages of Scripture is not meant to imply that there are other teachings found in the Bible that can address sexuality and even influence the conversation around homosexuality. My purpose here was to introduce you, or perhaps remind you, that there are differing views that should be considered as you seek to use the Bible to inform your views on sexuality or a sexual ethic, and to encourage you that exploring such views is incredibly valuable both for your own thinking as well as your conversations with others.

It's important to understand that differing theological opinions and debate are necessary for the health of the Church. Regardless of the side on which we find ourselves, we should desire to have sound interpretations as well as be willing to hear the critique of others. Allowing others to point out the flaws in your interpretations can help you solidify what you truly believe. However, it's equally important to see that when exposing flaws in interpretations becomes a means to put someone in their place, we have begun to dehumanize. Too often in this debate, though, we have used the Bible to deflate others, puff ourselves up, and point out the flaws in people's understanding or theological interpretations in order to prove they are wrong, unorthodox, or lazy. **Our Bibles deserve to be treated better than a weapon used to show others their faults.** The Bible, I believe, is not to be picked apart so that we can come up with a sexual ethic. Sure, there are parts of the Bible that can help us discern a sexual ethic. But the Bible is better than a sexual ethic. It's better than a list of dos and don'ts. It's better than a thing we use as a weapon to prove people wrong or to proudly establish ourselves as right.

My attempt here to represent both sides of interpretations in as unbiased a manner as I could, without entering into the debate, should not be taken to mean that I do not hold to a particular stance on sexuality.

It also doesn't mean I think such topics should not be debated, even debated in books. There are, in fact, countless books that do debate these things, in far more detail than I could—I have many of them on my bookshelves and recommend some of them in a reading list at the end of this book. The problem that I continue to see is that when we debate from a handful of passages whether or not homosexuality is right or wrong, our debates quickly become myopic, airless, distorted in their emphases above other Biblical truths, and detached from real people with real lives. When this happens, our debating becomes irrelevant, fruitless, or offensive. I believe that more often than not, we must step away from the debate, and toward relationships. This does not mean ignoring the debate, but instead means reframing it in the context of other truths and realities that help us see what is really at stake, which hopefully can bring a fresh resolution to it. The most fruitful and accountable context to have this conversation, I have found, is at the personal or local church level, and that is where I continue to have it. For it is in this community, where all are accepted, and where we out-grace one another by reminding one another that we are a family, where such robust and honest conversations can occur.

After so many deep and honest conversations with my close friend, Keith, I have come to conclude that when in relationship with another, his or her experience, personality, and theological understanding can be influencing. It actually makes studying the Bible more beautiful because I am reminded of the beauty that can be found in diversity. Whether Keith realized it or not, he encouraged me to study the Bible more, to fall more in love with it, to ask hard questions, to not accept easy answers, and to trust that God speaks through the Bible.

The Bible ultimately reveals God. The Bible is Good News. It shows us a God who loved people so much that He couldn't stay away from them. It tells the story of people trying to do godly things, often in ungodly ways. It reminds us of God's plan to restore, renew, and reconcile all things. It is worth reading and studying, and it has the power to transform us as we read it. My hope is that we will use the Bible not as a weapon to hurt others, but as a tool that transforms us into the likeness of Jesus.

5

CHAPTER FIVE

re-humanizing god's people

The previous chapter is where most scholars and Christians end the conversation on homosexuality. From my own study, I have seen how easy it is for us to debate those biblical texts until we are blue in the face, with little convincing. It saddens me how often we are divided on these texts, but what saddens me even more is that we often dismiss our fellow brothers and sisters in Christ because their opinion on homosexuality differs from ours. At times, I ponder how little the Bible talks specifically about homosexuality, yet how aggressively we debate it. I have spoken with people who have threatened to leave their church because it decided to welcome gay individuals. I have heard of others who have left a denomination because their theological standing on homosexuality has changed. There are people I know who, even though they have been friends for years, decide to dissolve the friendship because of their belief that homosexuality is sinful.

But what if we did better than divide? What if we entered a new conversation that took us away from trying to convince others of our viewpoints and instead discussed how we can remain united? This is the conversation I want to have. I feel this is my calling. Scholars can debate interpretations, but as a pastor, I feel it is my job to guide us into seeing Christ in one another and lead conversations that build people up, prepare people for acts of loving service, and point people to Jesus.

To be honest, I do not want to debate with my fellow believers in Christ about what the word *arsenokoites* really means, or whether Paul was speaking about pederasty. I think it is important for us to have open and honest conversations about such interpretations, which is quite different than a debate. I want to discuss if we can truly remain united and be an answer to Jesus' prayer to be one as He and God are one. With all my heart, I believe it is possible. With everything I have, I want to end dehumanization and division. With all that I am, I believe, united, we can show the world and our LGBTQ sisters and brothers, that the Gospel is truly Good News.

The Plight of Dehumanization

I remember the first time I watched the documentary *Trembling before G-D* by Sandi DuBowski, which takes a fascinating look at the stories of LGBTQ individuals within Judaism. In it, a rabbi argues that when people do not personally know gays and lesbians, it is easy to dehumanize them. However, when we know members of the LGBTQ community and have relationships with them, we are less likely to demonize and dehumanize.[65] I remember being overwhelmed by that simple, yet profound, truth. I have seen and contributed to the dehumanization of the broader LGBTQ community. At times, I have done so in ignorance or laziness, but regardless, I have contributed to it. Many Christians, as sad as it is, have shunned and ridiculed an entire group of people.

Yet, as I have been immersed in this topic for a while, I have also seen the LGBTQ and progressive Christian communities dehumanize and demonize the broader conservative Christian community. I, too, have been a part of this. I have labeled people as bigots or theologically dense. This is painful for all parties. I have come to believe that this dehumanization and division is utterly damaging to the mission God has given the Christian community.

There is no doubt about it—we dehumanize other people quite frequently. It has been our plight for a long time. A basic history course will remind us of all the atrocities that have occurred because humans have dehumanized others. We all have "removed the human-ness"[66] from another person and treated them poorly. We make assumptions about someone's personality or character and judge him or her in relation to our usually false assumptions. Ultimately, we end up believing that people are not created by God and do not deserve to be treated as such.

As a Christian, I have been convinced that all of humanity is the pinnacle of God's creation. Because of a well-known verse in Genesis, I believe that all humans are created in God's image: "Then God said, let us make humankind in our image, in our likeness... so God created humankind in his own image, in the image of God he created them; male and female he created them."[67] After the first humans were created, God exclaimed that creation was complete and considered "very good."[68] This reminds me that all people have the impression, imprint, and fingerprint of God upon them, and that all people, regardless of what they have done or will do, what they believe or what they will believe, where they have been or where they will go, have inherent worth and value. This is not because they have done anything to deserve it, but simply because they are created by God. It is who we are. **All humans are sacred and should be treated as such.**

I also believe that humans are flawed, and because of this, we dehumanize. Dehumanization is ultimately sin, and we all do it. Flawed women and men are good at pointing out the flaws of other humans. People are good at dehumanizing themselves and others. This is apparent in the story of The Fall, as it is known. Rather than being content with their humanity as created in God's image, man and woman wanted to "be like God."[69] This is the essence of sin. Sin is the desire to be like God, and our sinful actions flow from these desires. Sin is saying to God that we think we can be better at being God than God. It is trying to live life as if we are the center of the universe, acting as if we are God rather than living for God.

We see throughout Genesis 3 the consequences of sin and dehumanization. The first humans dehumanized one another as both denied their humanity, and in return, blamed one another for the mistakes they had made: "The man said, 'The woman you put here with me—she gave me some fruit from the tree, and I ate it.' Then the Lord God said to the woman, 'What is this you have done?' The woman said, 'The serpent deceived me, and I ate.'"[70] The man blames the woman and the woman blames the serpent.[71] They refuse to acknowledge their own faults and push the blame on another.

We still do this today. Recently, a fellow pastor of mine told me about the Fundamental Attribution Error. This is where we falsely attribute a particular action we do not think is correct to a flaw in someone's character. For example, if someone does not use their turn signal or cuts me off in traffic, it is very easy for me to attribute their mistake to their character. Perhaps I judge them to be lazy, ignorant, or a bad driver. However, if I happen to cut someone off in traffic, I usually blame my circumstances—I was in the wrong lane, I needed to get over very quickly, or I did not see them in my mirror. We falsely attribute blame or character to flaws without justification. This is dehumanizing.

As we continue in Genesis 3, we see that humanity begins to name and label one another. A verse that we often pass over, Genesis 3:20, says, "Adam named his wife Eve, because she would become the mother of all the living." In a quick reading, we think nothing about this verse. However, up to this point in the Genesis story, naming was only reserved for the animals.[72]

Naming can be incredibly powerful and encouraging. Yet, it can also be incredibly damaging and destructive. It can bring life, but it can also be used in negative ways to hurt others or to show dominance over another. If I am honest, I label and name people to feel better about myself or to show that I am more worthy than someone else. I think it is also fair to say we do this regularly to the LGBTQ community. We label and name, or we falsely attribute flaws to their character, and it is dehumanizing.

Dehumanization in Genesis 3-4 is full of blaming, labeling, naming, dominating, and murder. This is the spiral of dehumanization. Today, we continue to see dehumanization in countless ways, most of which can easily be seen in regards to class, race, and gender. We also see it with the LGBTQ community. Lesbian and gay individuals have been blamed, labeled, named, dominated, and even murdered.

The first thing we can do to stop such dehumanization and sin is to acknowledge it. We must understand that the dehumanization of the LGBTQ community, often perpetrated by Christians, has caused incredible pain, blatant inequality, self-hatred, internalized homophobia, and hostility. The paradox is that many Christians who believe they were created in the image of God do not see LGBTQ people as being created in God's image. They see gay individuals as inherently flawed or purposefully sinning, as if their orientation automatically trumps or negates their being made in God's image. They are seen by what they *do*, not by who they *are*. This, in and of itself, is dehumanizing, and it must stop.

When we are not in relationship with LGBTQ individuals, or with others who differ from us, it is easy not to view them as people created in God's image. It becomes easy to view those who differ from us as "them" rather than "we." Instead of loving the outcasts, marginalized, or "least of these," as Scripture has called us to do, we turn "them" into outcasts, marginalized, and "least of these," and have nothing to do with "them."

Both sides of this debate are guilty of this. The Christian community has often dehumanized LGBTQ individuals by viewing their actions as unholy or disgusting, while the LGBTQ community has often dehumanized the broader Christian community as bigots or homophobes. We have each turned those with whom we disagree into "others" and have ultimately given ourselves the license to think "others" do not deserve our love.

Our blatant lack of compassion is tiresome and inhibiting. We dismiss people as "others" if they do not agree with our theological convictions. If we are conservative and someone in our church believes homosexuality is not a sin, we often view him or her as a black sheep, theologically incorrect, or misled. If we are progressive and someone in our church believes homosexuality is sinful, we often view him or her theologically incorrect or misled. I have been labeled and named many things by Christians—from a rebel, to anti-Christ, to false teacher. Not too long ago, it was implied that I would be a heretic if I held a more progressive view of homosexuality.

CHAPTER FIVE

Recently, a friend and I were talking about how often we surround ourselves with people who think, look, act, believe, worship, and live just like ourselves. We then discussed how difficult it was for us to be in community with those we disagree with theologically. We easily view those who do not fit into our normative mold as "them" or as "other." My friend responded to this by saying, **"When we don't love 'them,' our love for God is a joke."**

For me, this was such a powerful reminder. At the time, I was frustrated with people who differed from me. I thought I knew the better way to worship, to disciple, or to serve the community. But my friend boldly reminded me that if I did not love them, I had no business claiming to be a follower of Jesus. As Thomas Merton commented on 1 John in his book, *Life and Holiness,* "Without our love and compassion for others, our own apparent love for Christ is fiction."[73] This is a clear reminder to me that I have a job to love God with all my heart, soul, strength, and mind. I also have the job of loving my neighbor as myself. If I do not intentionally engage in building relationships with others, my dehumanizing will continue, and my actions will be anything but reflecting the loving nature of Christ.

Jesus was in the business of re-humanizing all of creation. Jesus was all about re-humanizing those who had been marginalized and shunned. He reached out to women, befriended prostitutes, ate meals with sinners and drunkards, and made disciples of unlikely candidates. Jesus endured the utmost dehumanization so that we might never be dehumanized. Jesus was beaten and mocked, spit upon and executed, abandoned by His family and friends, and even forsaken by God, His Father, as He hung mutilated on a cross. **Jesus did it all in hopes for us to live a life where we refuse to dehumanize others.** Because of Jesus' life, death, and resurrection, God is reversing the spiral of dehumanization initiated in Genesis 3. God is returning all of creation back to Genesis 1, a place where humans are fully human, fully known, and fully loved. This is the Good News of the Gospel. All that was once dehumanized will be re-humanized yet again.

However, when we allow our thoughts and judgments to turn into actions, it almost always leads to division. When we make assumptions about people, such as calling them heretics or assuming they are deviant because of their sexual orientation, it becomes very difficult for us to remain in relationship with them. If we call someone a heretic, it is very easy to push him or her away. Left unchecked, dehumanization leads the Church to split and divide. I have seen it happen. Simply put, dividing is easier.

The Plight of Division

It is easier at times to divide. When people do not act like us, believe what we believe, or understand our experiences, it is easier to walk away. Of course, there are times in life when walking away from a particular community is healthy, safe, and appropriate. When certain communities are emotionally, physically, or spiritually damaging, it is fair to leave. However, when a community is divided over a particular viewpoint, it can be easier to walk away. This is because it is more comfortable to be surrounded by people like ourselves, being united in like-minded, homogenous groups. We know it is hard work to resolve conflicts, to view people not as their beliefs but as humans, and to remember that all humans, no matter their actions, are humans created in God's image. It is simply easier to divide.

For example, I am a staunch believer that women have been called and gifted to full participation and membership within God's Church. I maintain the belief that women should be affirmed to preach, teach, and pastor. Affirming women in ministry is not a liberal position but an orthodox and biblical position. At times, it has been hard to be in a community of fellow Christians who believe women should not be in such positions. At times, I find it easier to just leave. In my mind, it is even easier for me to believe they are ignorant, have not studied Scripture as thoroughly as I have, or that they are simply perpetuating misogyny. It is easier for me to dehumanize. It is easier for me to be an agent of division.

The Christian community has been fraught with divisions. **Sadly, rather than being known for our love, I think we are more often known for our divisions. This should grieve us.** We have divided into over 41,000 Christian denominations worldwide over non-salvific theological interpretations, political opinions, individual preferences of worship, or what gender is preaching from the pulpit. We contribute to division when we convict people outside our church walls, when we judge people who are not living the way we are, or when we feel suspicious of, or superior to, people who differ from us. We also participate in division when we force people to behave in a particular way before they can belong to our community.

Could it be that one of the reasons there is such a mass exodus of people leaving our churches is because we continue to divide? **Might it be possible that when people see Christians dividing, they cannot see God?** I wonder if people are hindered from seeing the Gospel when Christians constantly divide. In a culture that is rampant with division, from political parties to news stations, could unity among Christians be incredibly Good News?

What does this type of division do to the LGBTQ community? How can we be loving to them when we are hardly loving among ourselves? I do not think our division is attractive to the LGBTQ community. We are not a distinct community when we divide. We are living just like the world around us.

It is easier to dehumanize, easier to divide, but this does not make it the path we should take. Following the way of division is not the way of love. Division is sin, plain and simple. God hates it, for it goes against the essence of God. As stated earlier, Christians believe that God is triune— three in one. Because of this, there is perfect community in the Godhead. There is perfect harmony and unity among God, Jesus Christ, and the Holy Spirit. God is all about unity.

However, there is a force working against unity and God. In the Old Testament, this evil is called Satan, which is also translated as "enemy" or "adversary." Throughout the New Testament, Satan gets another name. We call the evil one the devil, which comes from the Greek word *diablo*, and can also be translated as "to destroy," "divide," or "tear apart."[74] This is the job of the enemy, the devil—to destroy, divide, and tear communities apart. It is what the devil does best. Whatever God seeks to unite, the devil seeks to rip apart. Whatever God seeks to keep together, the devil seeks to destroy. Whatever God seeks to weave together, the devil seeks to unravel. The mission of the devil is to divide. God loves unity because God is unity. **God hates division because it is the work of the devil.** The mission of God is unity.

Numerous verses throughout Scripture affirm God's love of unity and hatred of division. In the sixth chapter of Proverbs, the writer reminds the reader, "There are six things the LORD hates, seven that are detestable to him."[75] One of the seven detestable things is someone who stirs up conflict, discord, or disunity among the community of God's followers.[76] Disunity and discord are antithetical to God's nature and mission in the world. They do not have a place among God's people.

In his second letter to Timothy, Paul tells Timothy, "Keep reminding God's people of these things. Warn them before God against quarreling about words; it is of no value, and only ruins those who listen."[77]

Is it possible that our debating and quarreling about the words found in our Bibles about homosexuality might actually be causing ruin to particular people within our midst?

Gilbert Bilezikian's book *Community 101: Reclaiming the Local Church as Community of Oneness* has been most influential in shaping my thoughts on the importance of unity and community. In a powerful section,[78] his book reminds the reader of a poignant passage from Paul's letter to the Christians in Corinth, in which he asks the following question and reminds them of a bold truth:

> Don't you all know that you yourselves are God's temple and that God's Spirit dwells in your midst? If anyone destroys God's temple, God will destroy them; for God's temple is sacred, and you are that temple.[79]

I find this beautiful. Somehow, we become a temple where God dwells. This temple is sacred. We should not be destroying and dividing what is sacred. Even more, I want the LGBTQ community to experience the sacredness that is this temple, the Christian community. In fact, I want everyone to experience this, and I grieve when we, as this sacred temple, are a place of division rather than a place of love. I need a place full of love—I actually need it to survive. And, I think my LGBTQ friends need it, too. I hope they can find this within the Church.

The Holy Spirit is constantly working to unite people into a new humanity, a new community called the Church. One of God's aims is to glorify Himself through a united people and make God known to the entire world. Again, God no longer lives in a temple where people come to God. Rather, believers in Christ are now being united and built into a new humanity, a spiritual temple where God dwells. Now, God comes to the people through the people of God, and the message of God's salvation is made known to the world through the Church. God so loved the world that God gave the only Son (John 3:16), and the Son so loved the Church that He gave Himself up for Her. It is obvious to me that we need to do a better job of loving the Church like Christ did.

This is why unity is so important for the Christian Church. We believe when Christians gather together, God is present. We believe that when the watching world sees a reconciled group of people in relationship, they see a glimpse of God. We believe that when Christians are united together, people see the Gospel in action. This is why Bilezikian argues that when Christians divide, we actually give the world a reason to disbelieve the Gospel. For him, the proof that the Gospel is Good News and true is Christians being united and embodying Jesus' prayer in John 17.[80] This forces me to ask us, how does the LGBTQ community view us? Do they see us being beautifully united and embodying the Gospel? Or do they see us quarreling, stirring up conflict, and working with the devil to tear and divide?

Before He was executed, Jesus prayed for His disciples and for those who would believe in Him because of their message. The prayer is often called the Unanswered Prayer of Jesus, and it is found in the Gospel of John. After praying for His disciples, He said,

"My prayer is not for them alone. I pray also for those who will believe in me through their message, that all of them may be one, Father, just as you are in me and I am in you. May they also be in us so that the world may believe that you have sent me. I have given them the glory that you gave me, that they may be one as we are one, I in them and you in me, so that they may be brought to complete unity. Then the world will know that you sent me and have loved them even as you have loved me."[81]

Jesus' prayer for all of us who would become Christians was that we might be one and brought to complete unity so that the world will know that God loves them. What a powerful prayer! The Son of the Most High God prayed for us. His prayer was quite simple, yet profound. He prayed that we, despite our differences, might be one. Jesus knew that *if* we lived in such a way, the entire world would know that God loves them and sent them Jesus.

With all my heart and soul, I want to be a part of a movement of people who are living in such a way that through them, the world would know that God loves them. I want to live in such a way that my LGBTQ friends know God's love for them. I do not believe this is the current reality. From my experience, many of the LGBTQ friends have come to the belief that God hates rather than loves them.

Jesus prayed that we would be one, unified, found to be in complete unity. He prayed for His followers to be united because unity is the proof that the Gospel of

Jesus Christ is true.[82] We will love one another much deeper, and, because we are unified, we will look like heaven on earth. We will reflect and embody the unity of God in a divided world. This is such good news. **This is something I am willing to fight to achieve, and will lay down my life for it.**

It reminds me of the somewhat dramatic scene in the Pixar movie, Finding Nemo, when a massive amount of fish, including Dory, are trapped in a net being pulled up to a fishing boat. In spite of his dad's firm warning, Nemo knows the way to save all the fish. He eventually encourages the fish caught in the net to work together and swim downward. Over and over, they say, "Just keep swimming, just keep swimming!" Eventually, the force of hundreds of fish swimming downward causes the crane on the boat to break, allowing the net to open. All the fish find freedom and return to life in the sea.

The fish would not have survived as a group of individuals fighting for their own lives. The only way they had a chance of surviving was to work together. I wonder if we in the Christian community need to stop being so individualistic in order to survive. In essence, we need to be united and just keep swimming together. Think of how we can find much more freedom when we work for unity. When we resolve conflict, embrace our differences, understand our identity as children of the Most High God, and all start swimming in unity, there could be a freedom we have yet to experience. As Galatians 5:1 reminds us, it is for freedom that Christ has set us free.

As Christians and followers of the God who unites and brings peace, we pursue this unity so we're able to declare the praises of the God who called us out of darkness into His wonderful light. Christ gave Himself up for us and our LGBTQ sisters and brothers. Christ gave Himself up for the Church. He gave His life for Her to "make her holy, cleansing her by the washing with water through the word, and to present her to himself as a radiant church, without stain or wrinkle or any other blemish, but holy and blameless."[83]

We have some work to do. Our commitment to ecclesial unity must trump our non-salvific theologies, preferences, and opinions. **Because of the cross of Jesus Christ, we no longer have the right to divide**. Jesus divided the wall of hostility and the barriers that separated us by His body separated and pulled apart upon the cross. Through the cross, God has reconciled all people back to Himself. We no longer have the option of dividing when things get tough, ugly, or annoying. We no longer have the right to think ecclesial unity is some abstract idea. It is to be our reality. It is the way the world will know God sent Jesus and loves us.

Unity among Christians does not mean unanimity. There will be disagreements and differences of opinion. There is no doubt we need to be united on essential doctrines. We need to remain united around our faith in the life, death, and resurrection of Jesus Christ. Being united about who God is and what God has done for humanity is essential. Non-essential doctrines, such as those with numerous interpretations and opinions, we can freely differ. Fortunately, unity also brings with it diversity, and through diversity there can be powerful unity. The Bible reminds us that we must make every effort to be united. In the Epistles of Paul, we are reminded how crucial it is to lay down our own preferences and look to put the interests of others before our own so that we might remain together and united. Unity means that everyone can have a place at the table, everyone has a voice, and everyone is included because they are family. Paul also reminds us that we are a body. Each of us is a different part within this body, known as the Body of Christ. Paul says how ludicrous it is for the eye, for instance, to say to the hand, "I don't need you." Yet, in many Christian circles, we have said, in no uncertain words, to LGBTQ individuals, "We don't need you. You can't belong to the body." Paul reminds us, though, that when one part of the body suffers, we all suffer.

Let me also say, this is not going to be easy at all. For LGBTQ individuals, the calling to remain united in a church that does not affirm their sexuality seems impossible. And yes, for many conservative heterosexuals, it may be difficult to see married gay couples within the church community. However, the offensiveness of grace demands that we remain united, love one another, and be in relationship so we can find freedom. When we start swimming together, even though we are all different fish, we can find freedom and realize that we are all in this together, treating one another as Christ treated us.

6

CHAPTER SIX

holy moments

Coming Out as Holy Moments

The last few chapters have taken us through very deep, and possibly for some, challenging terrain. **We have seen how easy it is to come to opposing opinions about homosexuality using the same Bible.** We have spent a lot of time covering the theological components of this debate by looking at six passages of Scripture that often get interpreted in different ways. Sadly, our interpretations of these texts have been one of the reasons Christians have become divided over this topic. Even more so, these texts have been used to dehumanize people. Many of us have done so with those who disagree with us about homosexuality.

As we saw in the last chapter, though, Christ calls us to a better, albeit more difficult, way to live—the way of unity. If we are unified, as we are reminded in Jesus' prayer in John 17, then the world will know God is true. This is a high calling and one we should pursue with everything we have. My goal is now to move us away from simply talking about theology and remind us again of the humanness of this topic.

We have seen how the Bible can be used to bring about theological interpretations, personal opinions, and even hurt to others. But, the Bible deserves to be treated better than that. The Word can reveal to us the character and nature of God. As the Holy Spirit reveals the character of God, the Spirit transforms the reader into the likeness of Christ. Scripture is a tool that can transform the reader to passionately follow Christ and do good works for the Kingdom of God. My hope is that through this debate, we do not forget this point. We must study the Bible and know it, but most importantly, allow ourselves to be transformed by the One whom the Bible reveals.

The Bible leads us to Christ, and Christ leads us to people. Although we have spent a lot of time looking at the different opinions about homosexuality from Scripture, my hope is that we would be reminded that this is not a debate about six passages from the Bible. Instead, it is a conversation about God's children, men and women who are deeply loved by Christ and deserve to be treated as such.

More and more, we will know people who are gay. At some point, someone will "come out" to us. She or he will muster up the courage to reveal an aspect of his or her story and identity to us. We will then get to choose how we respond. In the coming pages, I want to encourage us to respond in a way that reflects Christ. As we do, we will remind people that their identity is, first and foremost, found in Christ. This identity in Christ is radically Good News. It is not something static or something we must work to attain and achieve; rather it is bestowed upon us. We grow up into this new identity.

Because of Christ Jesus, identity is not based on orientation. Identity does not come from being "gay" or "straight." It also does not come from one's career, failures, successes, family of origin, sins, or actions. LGBTQ individuals are not defined by their sin or actions. Instead, they are defined by Christ's actions. This is the Good News of Christianity.

Over the years, I have had numerous friends, family members, and acquaintances "come out" to me. In some cases, I was the first person to whom they bared their souls and shared this secret about their sexuality. There have been friends I always knew were gay but who did not come out to me until years into our friendship. I have had classmates and colleagues share their journeys of being gay Christians. Through hundred of emails, I've learned there are so many people who simply want someone to hear their story. Other people I know have come out on television or boldly in a Facebook post. Through all the stories and coming-out moments, mostly in one-on-one conversations, I have heard joys and struggles, seen tears and raw emotions, listened to words of anger and hope, and have looked people in their eyes as they have poured out their souls.

Through this, I have found that such moments are not necessarily a time to respond with abstract theological answers or opinions about homosexuality. In those moments, being present with those individuals, pastoring them, and caring for them is what's most important. The best response in such situations is to **embody a pastoral presence.**

I became aware of the need to embody a pastoral presence rather than teaching theology while working as a chaplain in a pediatric intensive care unit at a hospital. Although I had always preferred adult baptism to infant baptism, I am a part of a denomination that practices both. At the hospital, I was in a conversation about infant baptism with a teenage patient who was dying of cancer. She had just given birth to a boy, and unfortunately, his prognosis did not give him many weeks, let alone days, to live. Sitting in a room together, she asked me if I would baptize both her and her infant child. In that moment, all my abstract theology about why I thought adult baptism was "better" than infant baptism raced through my head. I had the opportunity to present to this young woman all the arguments in favor of adult baptism and respectfully decline her invitation to baptize her child. Or, I had the option to pastor these children.

In that moment, as this young woman sat in her wheelchair facing death, I chose to be pastorally present rather than stand on my abstract theology. It wasn't that my theology was thrown out the window, but as this young woman looked me in the eyes and asked for God's grace to be administered to both her and her dying son, I could only agree to baptize both of them.

The baptism ceremony ended up being beautiful. Her entire family was present as we crammed tightly around her and her child in their small intensive care room. This teenage girl was baptized in the name of God the Father, Jesus Christ the Son, and the

Holy Spirit. Her young child, whose eyes I had never seen open and who could barely move, surprisingly opened his eyes and looked at me as I baptized him. Two months later, after struggling to survive and regain health, both the young mother and her son died within a few days of each other.

This experience made me wonder if abstract theology could actually block God's grace from being granted. If I had simply responded to this teenager with my theology about baptism rather than caring for her spiritual needs, could I have hindered her and her child from experiencing the grace of God? In a similar way, when a child of God comes out, we must be careful to respond pastorally. This means that we should be listeners, people who hold back opinions to hear the journey and story of the person. We should do our best to point people to Jesus and remind them of their identity in Christ. Being careful not to block God's grace from being experienced, we respond first with mercy.

Coming out moments, I have concluded, are incredibly holy moments.[84] Often they are filled with God's grace and presence in a way rarely felt. It is holy when a person sits with you one-on-one and is utterly vulnerable. Those coming out are laying their hearts into another's hands, opening themselves up in radical ways, and revealing a deep part of who they are. Most likely, they have struggled alone concerning their sexuality for years. Many have probably done the biblical work we've done in previous chapters as well. In sharing that they are gay, they have had to muster great courage to overcome fear and risk rejection, all from the desperate longing to be loved for who they are.

I learned this through a good friend, Keith, who came out to me. As mentioned previously, Keith and I had been friends for numerous years. We both worked and lived together. We both had been raised in Christian families. We both had gone through difficult relationships and break-ups with women at similar times. Yet, for years, Keith hid his sexuality from me and put up a heterosexual mask.

One night, after being friends for a couple of years, Keith called me up and told me he was gay. He said he had always been gay and often dated women to cover up his sexuality in hopes that it would change him. He hadn't wanted me to find out on social media, so he decided to pick up the phone. After an hour of talking, we hung up and continued to remain close friends, almost as if nothing had changed.

It was not until six years after that phone call I learned Keith had been petrified to tell me he was gay, as he feared I would walk away from our close friendship once I found out. This had happened with other people in his family after he came out. People shunned him, stopped inviting him to family functions, and did not acknowledge his relationships. Keith honestly assumed that the phone call would be the last time we ever talked. He expected the relationship to end that evening. Looking back, it was an incredibly beautiful and holy moment for our friendship. That moment deepened and shifted our friendship in a new direction, and it has become a conversation we cherish.

A Word to Parents and Families

Over the years, I have received a lot of questions from parents asking for advice on what to do when their children come out. For many parents and family members, it is a scary and difficult conversation to have. Within families, it is often easier for an individual to come out to a sibling before coming out to his or her parents.

This is a very tough conversation for parents in particular. I know of many who have blamed themselves for their child being gay. Many have asked whether they did something wrong while parenting. I know of parents whose first response to their child was that he or she was sinful and acting in rebellion against God. Others refused to talk with their child, almost ignoring his or her presence. On the other hand, I know parents who hardly batted an eye when their child came out, since they knew he or she was gay and they were waiting for such a moment.

So parents and family members, here is my advice to you. These conversations can be difficult. Your emotions might overcome you. At times, you may feel utterly alone, not knowing where or how to process this news. You may have thousands of questions and feel you need answers. Let me remind you—you're not alone. Not only do you have your family and friends, who will hopefully support you in this process, but there are also other parents and even organizations available to help you through this journey. It will take time, but things can and will get better.

CHAPTER SIX

If or when your child comes out to you, it might be tempting to rattle off your thoughts about homosexuality, ask whether he or she is sure about this, or be and act shocked. It may feel as if you do not even know the child sitting before you. All these emotions are normal. However, I encourage you to fight those feelings, and instead, remember that he or she is your dear child—the infant you held so close, the toddler that finally began talking and walking, the child you dropped off for the first day of school, the teenager who overnight seemed to grow into an adult, and the one you love with all your heart. Then, do your best to **hold back the questions and, instead, listen to your child's experience**. He or she has likely been dealing with this internally for many years. He or she has already read, studied, and may know what the Bible says about homosexuality. This is not the moment to throw out verses or try to convince your child he or she is actually heterosexual. He or she needs this to be the moment to verbally process and express this journey to you.

Because of this, I encourage you to ask questions like, "How long have you known this about yourself? Has it been tough? Have you told others?" You might feel awkward or worried you may ask the wrong questions. That is okay. Ask with a gentle spirit and let your child share his or her soul with you. Allow yourself to listen more than you talk, and thank him or her for being so honest and open with you. Acknowledge that this was probably a difficult conversation to risk having with you.

I have heard story after heartbreaking story of parents who became so angry or upset during these conversations that it permanently damaged the relationship between child and parent. For the sake of unity and maintaining the relationship with your child, remind them of your love for them. If your child does not frequently hear the words "I love you" from you, let this be a time when he or she is assured of it. If you say it all the time, say it again. In this moment, you have the chance to model Christ's love, prove to them that mercy triumphs over judgment, embrace your beloved child, and cast away his or her fears by embodying love. **My prayer is that you would choose to show compassion rather than judgment.** It will benefit you and your relationship in the long run.

Once the conversation is over, you will enter a time of grief. This is completely normal. Most likely, since the day you learned you were going to have a child, and perhaps even before then, you have had dreams about your child. For decades, you most likely have been dreaming who they will become, whom they will love, or what they will accomplish. Many of those dreams will not match the reality you have just discovered. Therefore, the dreams you have had for your child will have to change. It is completely understandable that you will grieve, and you should take your time to do so. Eventually, you should be open to the process of creating new dreams for your child.

Whether you are a sibling or parent, you may feel the need to share the news with other people. Perhaps you need the space to verbally process or are simply overwhelmed and need an outlet. However, I would caution you from "outing" your child or sibling to others without permission—I have witnessed relationships suffer when someone does this. I understand this desire, but please believe that it is important for you to honor their privacy. Ask them if they would mind if you shared this news with anyone else. This builds respect and trust, both of which are needed in seasons such as these. If appropriate, you can encourage them to open up to other family members, and offer to be part of these conversations.

Allow your child, sibling, or friend to teach you during this time. Ask them questions, get to know them, learn from them, and seek to understand them in new ways. Do not abandon them or distance yourself. Instead, humble yourself. **For the sake of the relationship, show them grace and continue to show grace to yourself**. Additionally, find other people who have LGBTQ children or siblings. Do life with them. Learn from them. Let them support you so you can support your child. There are great organizations and non-profits that can be of support during this time.

Finally, pray for your child, sibling, or family member. I do not recommend praying that their sexual orientation will change, be healed, or even that they will find a loving partner. I know you may want to pray this and feel justified in praying such prayers. Instead, I would encourage you to pray more boldly and deeper than that. I challenge you to pray that they will know how vast, deep, high, and long the love of Christ is. Pray that they would not lose their faith, but that the pursuing love of God would overwhelm them. Pray that God will be their rock, foundation, and anchor. Pray that God will protect them, make His face shine upon them, and give them peace. Pray that their identity would be found solely in Christ. Through all this, I think you can have a wonderful relationship with your child.

A Word on Dating and Weddings

At some point in the future, your gay friend, coworker, sibling, or child might come to you saying, "Hey, I want you to meet my girlfriend" or "Dad, I'm getting married." This will be an entirely different conversation than what you might have experienced above. For some of you, this might be exciting and celebratory news. For others, hearing this news might be incredibly difficult and utterly confusing, and it may even weird you out. Since we know that sexual attraction is a component in dating relationships, it is common for our thoughts to wander to the bedroom and wonder what is going on behind closed doors. Discomfort over sexual acts between people of the same sex can produce thoughts of disgust for some, thoughts that can easily be projected over a same-sex couple. Endeavor to give a same-sex couple the same privacy you would give any couple, and focus instead on acknowledging the companionship or emotional connection evident in the relationship.

When you hear your friend or family member is planning to get married, you may immediately recall why you do not believe in same-sex relationships or believe that gay men or women should be allowed to marry. Also, you may find yourself even wrestling with whether you should attend their wedding. It's possible to ask yourself if it is appropriate to attend a wedding when thinking homosexuality is sinful. Furthermore, you may wonder whether attending a wedding would be affirming the relationship.

My answer to whether or not a Christian should attend a gay wedding is always an emphatic yes. For an LGBTQ individual, the day of their wedding might possibly be one of the best days of his or her life. As it is for many heterosexuals, a wedding ceremony is a pinnacle event in their relationship—they look their best, they are joyful, and love is physically evident. Attending such an event allows you to participate in one of the most important days in a person's life.

Now, there have been times in my own life where I have attended a wedding of a friend, or even participated in the ceremony, and have not approved of the wedding or ensuing marriage. There were times where I questioned whether the couple was a good fit, whether they were emotionally and spiritually prepared for marriage, and whether they were truly happy, loved one another, or just felt pressure to get married. Even though I may not have agreed with the wedding, I still stood with them during one of the most important days in their lives. Attending a gay wedding allows you to show hospitality, to stand with people even if you do not affirm them, participate in their journey of love, and be in community with a diverse group of people supporting love. Standing with someone does not mean, for instance, affirmation.

I think Jesus gives us a great example of this in John 8[85] when He is approached by a group of Pharisees who had caught a woman in the act of adultery.

Because she was caught in a sinful act, the Pharisees believed she should be stoned, and they asked Jesus if He agreed with the Law, which allowed the stoning. Jesus responded to this mob by stating that those who were without sin should be the first to cast a stone. All the men dropped their stones and left; only Jesus and the woman remained. He then said to her, "Neither do I condemn you, go now and leave your life of sin."[86] Jesus stood with this woman when everyone else wanted to condemn and kill her. Everyone else in the story did not affirm this woman and refused to stand with her. They saw her only by her sinful actions. But Jesus saw her as a woman, a woman worth standing with and for.

Jesus said "leave your life of sin" to the woman because he's Jesus. He has the authority to say this. In this scene, Jesus literally saved this woman's life. According to the Law of Moses, she was to be put to death right there. Yet, Jesus literally saved her from death, and because of His life, future death, and resurrection, He saved her from all her sin. Jesus had the authority to speak in such a way.

Jesus also rebuked all those who were passing judgment on the woman. My guess would be that today, Jesus could say the same to us when we try to pass judgment on others for actions we do not affirm. It is true; Jesus told the woman to leave her life of sin. Yet, before He said that, He lovingly said, "Neither do I condemn you." That is the beauty of grace. That is the model by which we should live.

Many people throw this passage around in the debate about homosexuality. Because Jesus said, "Go and leave your life sin," we often say the same thing to LGBTQ individuals. We say this so simply and flippantly—"leave your life of sin." Do we really think that the woman caught in adultery sinned no more? Most likely, she did sin. And so do we. Even after a life-saving encounter with God, we go away and sin. The beauty, though, is that God continues to find her, love her, and tell her to keep going. God continues to find, love, and tell us to keep going. Even after I have incredible encounters with God, I go away and sin. Yet, when I do, I continue to remember that the God of Love who pursues me and says, "I do not condemn you. I love you. Keep going."

Sadly, I have seen many relationships sever or develop major crack when people vehemently oppose going to a gay wedding or decide to throw the first stone. Many of those relationships break down and build up barriers when people decide to say such words as "leave your life of sin." In my opinion, the day you get a wedding invite or are at the wedding rehearsal is not the moment to go on a rampage about your theological beliefs. All I have seen it do is hinder relationships from continuing, put up barriers, and block meaningful conversations.

Just as there are different interpretations on the biblical scholarship pertaining to homosexuality, there are also different interpretations pertaining to gay weddings. For some religious denominations and individuals, gay marriage is openly celebrated and affirmed. Pastors and religious leaders in these settings can freely officiate any type of wedding, encourage LGBTQ individuals to get married, and open their church doors to such celebrations. On the other hand, there are religious denominations and individuals that renounce gay marriage, viewing it as unbiblical or not what God intended. Pastors and religious leaders in these settings are unable to officiate gay weddings and may not encourage others to participate. There are also differing opinions over the term "marriage." For some, it is strictly to be between one man and one woman. For others, a marriage can be between two people who are committed to one another for life. You may find that your definition of marriage might be different than those whom you witness getting married.

When the day comes for you to think about going to a gay wedding, I would encourage you to pray—a lot. I would also encourage you to ask what loving like Christ looks like. Does it mean attending a wedding ceremony of a friend or family member, even if you do not agree with the marriage? Can you stand with someone, even if you do not affirm her or his actions? How can you look like Christ and love them like Christ? I would also encourage you to read books by pastors and scholars who have written about different perspectives on gay marriage and how Christians can respond. My hope is that our response to a wedding announcement is drenched in love, mercy, and grace.

A Word to Pastors and Ministry Leaders

I was having a discussion with a pastor colleague and mentor of mine recently on the subject of homosexuality. We were discussing one-on-one pastoral care settings and what to do when a person enters our office for pastoral care. Often, within the first few minutes, a person may share why they are there. It could be that they are gay, addicted to porn, struggling to hear from God, in great pain, grieving, discouraged, or even questioning the legitimacy of Christianity. As pastors, our job is to listen, remind them of their identity in Christ, point them to God, and encourage them with the Gospel.

Sometimes, though, our pastoral care can be riddled with catchphrases or cliché pastoral responses. I hope we move away from defaulting to such answers and instead help people draw near to God. Our pastoral care need not answer every question nor fix someone's situation. We do not need to constantly correct or even discipline. At times, our pastoral response is not sitting in an office answering tough theological questions.

More often, our care should direct people to God, the Bible, and prayer. It should be a time where we listen deeply to the needs and honest words that are voiced, then express gratitude, boldly encourage, and graciously remind. This shows our commitment to their well-being. As one of my mentors has always reminded me, we should love our congregants more than we want to convict, convert, or even persuade them of proper doctrine. We should commit to doing life with them, doing spiritual practices with them, and even "getting in the mud" with them, so to speak, so that they might know we will care for them well.

Many an individual has walked into my office or shared over a cup of coffee that he or she is gay or lesbian. There have been times where I have been tempted to respond with a denominational stance on homosexuality. Early on, there was a moment of panic, as I was not sure of the best way to respond. Sometimes, it felt as if I were blindsided, completely unprepared for the conversation taking such a turn.

Yet, hundreds of conversations later, I not only welcome such dialogue, but also feel prepared, equipped, and excited to journey with people as they come out to me. This is why the first words that usually come out of my mouth when someone else comes out are words of gratitude. As I said earlier, coming-out moments are holy moments. Therefore, I think it is imperative to thank people for being vulnerable, brave, courageous, and open to share a part of their soul. As with all pastoral care, we respond to the emotions shared; we listen for the hurt, pain, and other experiences that have been encountered. **We should empathize more than we sympathize.**

Often in these conversations, after someone says, "I'm gay," I ask him or her, **"What type of gay person do you think God wants you to be?"** This allows for conversation to continue and for me to learn some of the process and journey through which this congregant has been walking. I have found most people have a pretty clear answer to this question, which can allow you as a pastor to shepherd them toward Scripture and prayer. After asking this question, conversations have veered into the topics of holiness, reading Scripture, doing justice, and moving beyond simply talking about a sexual ethic. I love this question because it also allows the conversation to be much more collaborative than if I simply tell them what they should do. It allows me to enter into their journey rather than assuming I know where their journey is going.

In addition to expressing gratitude and asking the above question, I also say, "I'm sorry," when needed. Apologizing, as we saw with the corporate apology at the 2010 Chicago Pride Parade, can be a tool to bring reconciliation and understanding, and can also allow for deep conversation. Apologizing and thanking the person for his or her vulnerability and trust are ways of telling a congregant "You matter." Many have told me, to my shock, that they never expected to hear a pastor say, "Thank you," "I'm sorry," or "I don't know" in response to someone coming out or discussing the topic of homosexuality. Hearing these words actually enables them to humanize a pastor, which allows trust to be built. It also allows us the freedom from having to live up to being the know-it-alls.

If in this conversation you are going to encourage a particular type of living for LGBTQ people such as celibacy, chastity, abstinence, or even monogamous relationships, you must have systems and settings within your congregation in which such living can actually occur. If you require celibacy for LGBTQ Christians, for example, your church must graciously provide a setting where the congregant's emotional, physical, and spiritual needs can be met so that they may successfully live a celibate life. It also means you need to create an environment where they may openly confess, share their longings, and ask for help without feeling shamed, guilty, or as if they were second-class citizens. It's fair to say our congregations need to do better in this area in general.

In addition to this, I would recommend that you continue to follow up with LGBTQ Christians within your church. Ask them what systems or structures would benefit their daily Christian living within your congregation. Resource them as best as you can. There are great organizations, such as the Gay Christian Network, The Marin Foundation, New Directions, The Reformation Project, and the Christian Closet that can help in your pastoral care.

Another thing I would encourage you to consider is your church's requirements and policies for membership. As we've discussed in previous chapters, people are looking for a place to belong, and your church has the chance to create a space where they can find love, mercy, and grace. In a safe place of belonging, people are able come to belief in God and, eventually, become devoted disciples of Christ. Perhaps your church has LGBTQ individuals in attendance. They may sit under your preaching and teaching, participate in communal worship, partake of weekly communion, volunteer in different capacities, and freely give of their tithes and offerings, yet they are not welcomed into full membership. When LGBTQ people are serving your church, giving their time and energy to live out the mission and vision, or donating their finances but are not members, they are not being served. They are being used.

I understand that this may cause some pushback from some of you, as it may seem unthinkable to consider LGBTQ membership. Regardless, I do think it is worth your time to evaluate your membership policy with your pastoral staff, elders, or leadership team.

CHAPTER SIX

As pastors and leaders within your ministry context, I hope that you would proactively serve your people by asking the following questions: Are there particular actions or ways of living that preclude people from being members in your church? Is being attracted to someone of the same sex a disposition that automatically means one cannot be a member? If we are all considered sinful in one way or another, why are some sins barriers to membership while others are not? Are there any passages of Scripture that help you form your requirements for membership, and how might those texts influence your discussion of potential LGBTQ members? Finally, for any people seeking membership, what part does radical grace play in determining whether or not they can be members in your congregation?

One final opportunity your pastoral care can provide is the gracious teaching of theological beliefs and interpretations about a myriad of topics. Therefore, teach your denomination's theological teachings. While I was ministering in college ministry, I would ask students which denomination they were a part of so that I could learn what their church of origin usually taught on sexuality. I would share my own denomination's stance. Then, and I believe it is completely fair to do so, I would quickly teach the entire spectrum of belief in regards to sexuality. I did this because I found most people are quite illiterate about what the Bible says about sexuality, as well as the scholarly work that has been done on the subject. This gives your congregants a well-rounded approach and understanding of the topic as they continue to live out their faith.

Finally, as I have mentioned in every other section, pray. Be intimately connected to the Source in whom we live and move and have our being. Beg God for mercy, the Spirit's discernment, grace and mercy that constantly triumph over judgment, and love that is patient and kind. Pray that over all virtues, God will clothe you, and your congregants who are LGBTQ, with love, which binds everything together in harmony. Pray that they might know the Gospel, the Good News of Jesus Christ, in new and fresh ways, so that you all might have the power, with all the saints, to grasp how wide, and long, and high, and deep the love of Christ is.

A Word to LGBTQ Individuals

I do not know how many of my LGBTQ sisters and brothers will pick up a book like this, but I feel I must address you as well. In the numerous conversations I have had with my LGBTQ friends and family members, I have been amazed by your stories, journey, struggles, pain, and sorrows. There have been times in such conversations when I have said the wrong things, been insensitive and rude, and simply been ignorant in my responses. I'm thankful that you have been so gracious to me as I have journeyed with you into your community. I believe Christians can learn so much from your community. You have taught me how to embody love, acceptance, and resilience.

I am also sorry a book like this has to be written. I am sorry for how often you have been dehumanized. I am sorry some people view you with disgust and dismiss you rather than seek to understand you. I am chagrined that many pastors and preachers have taught that you are the cause of 9-11 or natural disasters, and I apologize that some Christians believe them. I am sorry you have been taught to believe that God is mean, cruel, or distant because Christians have acted in mean, cruel, and distant ways. I am sorry that we have viewed you more by your orientation than by your humanity, and that judging you and your community has become commonplace among Christians. Please forgive us that we have not been Christ-like to you.

I know that we, as Christians, do not deserve your forgiveness, but I plead that you would be gracious and merciful to us. Please treat us more like Jesus than we have treated you. I know you deserve justice and retribution, but I would ask that you surprise us. Be gracious to us and love us. I believe that when you do, the Christian community will better know God's grace and realize the utter hurt they have caused you. I believe we would be compelled to repent and confess our sins against you.

After having so many conversations, hearing many coming-out stories, and learning about your community, I hope to remind you of a few things as a pastor. I ask you to be gracious and patient even when you do not feel like it, even when others do not deserve it, and even when it seems impossible to do so. For the sake of maintaining any relationship, whether with a family member or friend, you must be gracious and patient with those to whom you have come out. After coming out to friends or family members, it can be very easy to be discouraged, impatient, and even willing to

dismiss them. You might even have every right to distance yourself from certain family members or friends.
At times, that distance from harmful or emotionally
damaging relationships is completely acceptable and
needed. However, because a family member is theologically conservative or disagrees with you does not
justify ending a relationship. For the sake of maintaining a relationship, remember that many of us are not
as far along on this journey as you are. Be patient. You
have had years of wrestling, questioning, thinking,
praying, and figuring out a huge aspect of your identity.
However, your parents, friends, family members, and
others you have come out to are just starting that journey. So, be gracious to us.

As we begin the journey, which you have been on
for much longer, we may say ignorant things, make
you mad, ask inappropriate questions, and offend you.
However, if you want us to understand you, support
you, be a champion for you, or even be in favor of gay
rights, guide us. We need you to lead us in that.

After coming out to parents, the relationship
between the child and the parent often reverses in
some ways. The parent, like a child, may throw temper
tantrums, be aloof at times, or ask the same question
over and over. As the child, you now have the chance
to parent your parent. Please teach them, be patient
with them, lead them, answer their questions no matter
how often they ask, and guide them to understanding.
Love them, even if they don't deserve it. Parent them
through this.

I say this because I have seen those who parent
their parents maintain relationships and have seen

incredible examples of reconciliation and restoration. There are parents who struggled with their child's sexuality but became their child's anchor, support, and champion. Some parents mentor other parents who have just started on this journey. I also know of parents who would normally dehumanize work through things to humanize their child again. The work is hard and at times may seem impossible, but I believe the work will be worth it.

These same guidelines and needs have applied to my own relationships with my friends of a different race or ethnicity as we have pursued racial reconciliation and deep friendship. In my relationships with my African American or Asian American friends, for example, I have needed them to be patient and gracious with me and guide me to an understanding of my own white privilege, racial biases, racially ignorant comments, and insensitivity. If they dismiss me after my first racially biased comment or my false assumptions that racism is not a problem in our culture, our friendship will collapse. If I dismiss them for their frustration with white privilege or their impatience with me as I try to understand systemic racism and white supremacy, our friendship will fall to pieces. However, if we commit ourselves to the pursuit of racial reconciliation, understanding, and friendship, our relationship will only flourish and stand the test of time.

If you have yet to come out, it can also be good to make a coming-out plan. The coming-out process does not need to happen at one time on a social media post or a large public announcement. As I have counseled individuals as they come out, many have decided to slowly come out to different family members or friends over a period of time. For instance, one friend of mine told her three closest friends and roommates. After there was understanding and conversations in those relationships, she then decided to tell a handful of family members. Another gentleman I know planned his coming-out process over a six-month period, which included telling his closest friends, family members, coworkers, and pastor.

Therefore, I recommend taking your time coming out to people. It's always better to do this conversation face to face, even if it is much more intimidating and scary. Come out to those individuals who matter to you, to those whose friendships you cherish, and to those family members whose relationship you want to maintain. Then, once those conversations go well, and when you feel comfortable and secure, broaden the coming out process. You may find that there are some people you never tell, and that is okay. The entire universe does not need to know your sexual orientation. It is not your entire identity but an aspect of who you are. Therefore, share with those people you want to know.

One other important piece of advice for LGBTQ individuals journeying with family members or friends during this coming-out process: **live a life that proves stereotypes wrong**. Especially among some conservative individuals, being gay can bring to mind countless stereotypes and dehumanizing thoughts. Therefore, live a life that proves them wrong.

If you are a Christian, this means pursuing holiness in all areas of your life. Being out, as a Christian, does not give you the option of living a promiscuous life or any way you choose. Holiness and living like Christ cannot get thrown out the window simply because you are out. Unfortunately, the bar is set higher for you. This is because some individuals will blame certain actions upon your sexual orientation. For example, if your drinking gets out of control and you get drunk, some people may say that you are heading down a dangerous spiral and blame it on your orientation.

As unfair or frustrating as it may be, you have to prove to certain people that you are not some deviant, sex addict, or evil person. Live above the stereotypes they have. Live a life that proves to them you are human. Live a life that shows you are more than your orientation. Live a life like Christ.

Although there is no way I can completely relate to what you might be going through, or will be going through, I do know that you are not alone in this. I know the journey can be tough, that you might feel like giving up, and that things might get so hard that you feel like running away from it all. I know that at times thoughts of suicide have raced through your mind. For some of you, you may feel like giving up on this whole faith thing entirely. You may want to throw in the towel and turn your back against Christianity and God. I understand that and can see why you would want to give up.

Let me plead with you for one second as a pastor in the Church. Do not give up on Jesus. You might feel like giving up on Christianity or certain Christians, but don't give up on Jesus. He is the image of the invisible God, the Author and Perfector of your faith, the One who pursues and loves you dearly, and the God who likes you. Christians are not perfect, and I know many of them may not have treated you in a positive manner. But Jesus is perfect, and His perfect love casts away all fear. Do not give up on Jesus, for Jesus has never given up on you. He knows the number of hairs on your head. He knit you together in your mother's womb. He rejoices when you turn to Him, and as He hung on a cross with all sin upon His shoulders, He knew your name and did it all for you. The cross is the reminder that you matter. The empty tomb is the reminder that you can have life to the fullest. Jesus has not forsaken you, and will not forsake you. Do not give up on Him.

Finally, pray. Draw near to God. Let God be your guide as you guide others. Let God be your parent as you seek to parent others. Let God be your strength when you have none. Let God hear your cries. Let God be your anchor. Let God be your identity. Remember, you do not travel this alone. Our God is Emmanuel, God with us, and God with you.

CONCLUSION:

the time is now

Rick took me under his wing during our years at college, and I was grateful for his friendship. He possessed a wealth of knowledge, especially random trivia about musical theatre. Rick knew facts about Elaine Stritch and Carol Channing they did not even know themselves, or so it seemed. He enjoyed performing and directing, and was skilled beyond belief in costume design. We were in many classes together during our years at college. We also were roommates for a couple years, and even studied theatre for a semester in England. It was my friendship with Rick that eventually eliminated all the ignorant stereotypes I had of gay individuals.

I looked up to Rick, whether he knew it or not. I hoped I could be as skilled and knowledgeable as he. His identity as a costume designer and as a young man seemed to be so secure. Rick was naturally and effort-lessly extroverted, with an extraordinary, memorable laugh. People just wanted to be around him, myself included. For years, Rick was one of my closest friends. Through his friendship, along with a handful of others at college, I was welcomed into a community of people who I saw as family, who I cared for deeply, who were better friends to me than I was to them, and who I remember fondly. I am thankful that we still can main-tain a friendship, even if life has taken us in different directions, places, and careers.

One year, Rick and I managed to secure a four-per-son suite in the dorm just for ourselves. I am not sure how we finagled the acquisition, but I was excited to score a sweet dorm for a year with him. While in my hometown for the winter break, I was explaining the roommate situation to a high school friend, Leslie, who also attended the church I had been a part of grow-ing up. Leslie knew that Rick was gay and proceeded to ask me if I had evangelized him to accept Christ and become heterosexual.

In that moment, it seemed she was telling me it was more important to try to convert Rick to our faith than to develop a friendship with him. I felt as if she viewed him as less than, simply because he did not verbally profess our shared belief. I avoided fully answering Leslie's question. I said I was simply his friend, and we did not talk about Jesus too often.

If I Had Known

It was true that I did not evangelize Rick. I was never a fan of proselytizing. At that point in my life, evangelism had been presented to me as some obligatory and manipulative way to control a conversation, and frankly, I did not want to use my friends in order to talk about Jesus. In college, I still believed Christianity to be a behavior-based gospel, where behaving a certain way was the way to gain God's acceptance. I did not share my faith often because I questioned how such a gospel was truly Good News.

I wish I had known the beauty of the Gospel back then. I probably would have shared it with friends much more regularly. Christianity, as I have come to learn, is so much better than manipulating conversations to talk about God. It is so much better than thinking I am better than others simply because I know Jesus. The Good News is better than that. It's better news than I could ever imagine. I'm thankful that Christianity is more than just trying to work hard to be blessed by God.

At times, it makes me wonder what the churches I had been a part of were actually preaching. It wasn't the Good News I know now. I now see that the Gospel announces that God loved us so much that He couldn't stay away, but drew near to us in the person of Jesus Christ. Jesus loved us so much that He gave all He had, His own life, so we may experience God, who is love. This God in the flesh was punished, beaten, executed, and even separated from God so that we might never be abandoned or forsaken. The Gospel announces that Jesus physically rose from the dead, conquering evil, sin, death, and the devil and reconciling or uniting us to God and one another. The Gospel is the reminder that we do not have to earn our way to God, but rather that God comes to us.

In the Book of Leviticus, we learn that the lame, poor, blind, and disfigured could not approach God. These people were considered unclean, unholy, or sinful. I was taught that gay people fell into a similar category. And yet in the Gospels, Jesus, God in flesh, not only approached, but also ate dinner with the lame, the poor, the blind, and the disfigured. I therefore conclude that Jesus would eat dinner with gay people, and probably hug a gay man at a Pride Parade. Jesus overturned the rules. He went against what was always done. He is scandalously inviting and inclusive. The Gospel reminds us that God approaches and pursues us. This Gospel is expansive; it's deep and wide, and it truly is the best news the world will ever hear.

I wish I had shared this news with Rick. I wish I could have told him he did not have to get cleaned up or straight to know God's love. I imagine I said ignorant and offensive things to him. Many times, I was the hypocritical Christian, and he saw that reality. I wish I had told him that his way of loving and accepting me was the same way God accepts him.

With my Bible verses hanging on my bulletin board and my leaving for church early on Sunday mornings, Rick must have known I was a Christian. But I hope he knows I felt it was never my job to convict or even convert him. I hope through our friendship he saw a different side of Christianity than we were both taught to believe. It was Rick who actually taught me about God. It was Rick who reminded me what it means to love without strings attached. This is how Jesus loves all of us, without conditions.

Grace is the beauty and touchstone of Christianity. For some people, though, it can be very offensive. Grace can be offensive to those of us who think we are entitled to it. You see this in the Parable of the Workers in Matthew 20. "Are you envious because I am so gracious?" the text asks. When we think we are entitled to grace, the extension of grace to someone else seems outrageous. Yet, to the one to whom grace is extended, it is a breath of fresh air. Our job as Christians is to be vessels of grace rather than becoming angry or manipulative when someone freely receives grace. We are to bring fresh air to those longing for it.

At times, I wonder if my gay friends will ever return to the Church. I wonder if they will ever see the beauty in the invisible God made flesh in Jesus. Many of them were raised in Christian homes, found a community among Christians, and fell in love with the God of Love. Yet, after coming out, usually due to the way in which Christians treated them, they left their Christian homes, left the Christian community, and gave up on God. This is unacceptable.

Do we prefer that our fellow sisters and brothers leave? What about the words of St. Paul that say when one member suffers, we all suffer? We cannot say to another part of the body of Christ, "I have no need for you," or "there is no space for you here," or "you cannot belong here." Our sisters and brothers who happen to be LGBTQ are suffering. Much of it comes from our own words and hands. Sadly, we are all suffering because of it.

What About Tristan?

Over the years, I have wondered about Tristan, the gentleman I hugged at that Gay Pride Parade. Christians have wounded him so much that he wants nothing to do with the Church or Christian community, and it saddens me. He has been quite hostile toward Christians because I believe Christians have been quite hostile towards him. I do not know whether Tristan will ever enter a church building or form deep friendships with Christians. As sad as it may be, I believe Christians have pushed him so far from God that he may never turn back to God.

For the rest of our lives, Tristan and I will share a bond—a hug at a Gay Pride Parade that went viral. However, I hope that it was more than just a hug. I hope that somehow Tristan caught a glimpse of the Jesus I believe to be true and real. I have, at times, done a poor job of reflecting Jesus to those around me. The freedom, acceptance, and love that Tristan and others experience at a Gay Pride Parade can, I hope, one day be an experience within the Church. Sadly, it might be too late for Tristan and others. We might have lost our opportunity to represent Christ to them.

Think about that for a moment. Our actions as Christians may have pushed many LGBTQ individuals to give up on God. They refuse to have anything to do with God, not because of who God is, but because of how Christians behave. Let that sink in deep. This should grieve us, disgust us even, and fill us with righteous indignation to change that reality. Some of us have represented Christ so poorly to the LGBTQ community that they actually believe God hates them. That alone should make us put this book down, fall prostrate before God, and beg for forgiveness. Then, when we get back up, it should compel us to do whatever it takes to confess our sins, pursue reconciliation, and make changes to our church communities.

Knowing the beauty of God's bride, the Church, I do believe Tristan is missing out not being a part of the Christian community. In it, I believe he could find grace, truth, love, and mercy like never before. I can also say that I think the Christian community is missing out because Tristan is not a part of it. When I think about my friends who happen to be gay and picture each of them, I am almost brought to tears knowing that they are not part of God's Bride, the Church. Rather than being included and welcomed into a community of Christians, they have been shunned and driven to form a community outside the Church. I want nothing more for them to stand with me in the pew as we worship the risen Jesus together. The Church will be better when they are invited in and embraced.

It is time something changes. Our loving actions must trump our abstract passivity. Mercy must always triumph over judgment, and grace must abound more than our phobias. It is time we pursue reconciliation. We cannot avoid this topic any longer. It is long overdue to begin fruitful dialogue on what can often be a scary topic. We have to engage it because we are in relationship with others.

I no longer want it to be the norm that LGBTQ individuals are giving up on God because we have given up on them. God calls the Church to look out for the marginalized. Whether we accept it or not, the LGBTQ community has become marginalized from our churches. I am tired of hearing stories of people like Tristan who have been so hurt by Christians and given up on God. It is time we seek them out, confess our sins, ask for forgiveness from them, and prove to them that God loves them. It is time we show Christ's love. The Gospel, the Good News of Christianity, is at stake.

May we all be encouraged to speak the truth that our LGBTQ sisters and brothers in Christ are beloved children of the Most High God. I believe we must remind them that there is nothing that can separate them from the love of God found in Christ Jesus. Because of Jesus' life, death, and resurrection, God now views them, and us, holy in His sight, without blemish and free from accusation. God does not love some future cleaned-up version of them, but loves them right where they are. Scripture reminds us that God knows every hair on their head. He lovingly knit them together in their mother's womb, knows when they stand up and sit down, knows when they are in the deepest valley or the highest mountain, knows when they are in need, and draws near to them when brokenhearted.

My challenge is not to stir up conflict or division, but I challenge all of us to pursue unity no matter the cost. We have a high calling—to be vessels for mercy and grace, not judgment. We must be agents who help bring about God's Kingdom on earth rather than hinder it. We must be on the side of God, the One who unites, rather than on the side of the devil, who seeks to divide and destroy. We need to be so in love with the Good News of Jesus Christ that we would share it with all people, knowing that we cannot mess up God's Kingdom. Not even the gates of Hell will prevail against it, so surely our non-salvific theologies do not have the power to either.

What would it look like if we became such a community? What if we were so gracious that people were shocked at our inclusive spirit? What if we were so welcoming our churches began to bust at the seams? What if we were so unified that we became a diverse mosaic of people who resembled the Kingdom of God on earth? What if we said like Jesus, "Come, all who are weary and heavy laden, and Jesus will give you rest?" What if we did whatever it took to keep the unity of the Spirit through the bond of peace? What if we lived as a family, created in God's image to bear God's image, who loved so well that all fear is cast out and all people know we are God's disciples? What if we were one as Jesus and God the Father are one so that people will know that God sent Jesus? I would want to be a part of that. I think all people would want to be a part of that. For that would be a glimpse of heaven on earth.

It is time to journey with God's beloved and diverse children, even when we disagree with God's beloved and diverse children. It is time we lean on the side of being overly gracious, welcoming, and loving. I would rather risk making the mistake of being overly gracious and inclusive so that they may know Christ, than be indifferent and exclusive, risking them not knowing Christ. Even if all our interpretations and conclusions are wrong, I trust God is big enough to handle our mistakes. We must embrace love, for Love always embraces us.

AMEN.!

Holy and Compassionate God,

Bless with Your abiding presence our sensitive, loving, and faithful friends, those whose loneliness is deep and dark by virtue of their being misunderstood and rejected. Knowing that the issue of sexual identity too easily leads to the hasty prejudice of others and sorrowful self-judgment, in the name and power of Your Son Jesus, who had unusual and unconditional love for those often ostracized and moved to the margins of the culture of His time, bring Your refreshing and healing Spirit to those persons whose soul and heart have embraced Your saving grace but find Your church and society unkind and demeaning. And help us to keep reminding them that they are dearly loved by us and by You. Amen.[87]

RECOMMENDED READING

Achtemeier, Mark. *The Bible's Yes to Same Sex Marriage: An Evangelical's Change of Heart.* Louisville, Kentucky: Westminster John Knox Press, 2014.

Albert, Nathan. *Belong, Believe, Become: The Evangelical Covenant Church and Homosexuality.* Chicago: North Park Theological Seminary, 2011.

Albert, Nathan. "I Hugged a Man in His Underwear. And I am Proud." *It Seems to Me…*, http://naytinalbert. blogspot.com/2010/06/i-hugged-man-in-his-underwear-and-i-am.html (accessed January 25, 2015).

Alexander, Marilyn Bennett, and James Preston. *We Were Baptized Too: Claiming God's Grace for Lesbians and Gays.* Louisville, Kentucky: Westminster John Knox Press, 1996.

Anderson, Glenn. *Covenant Roots.* Chicago: Covenant Press, 1999.

Bilezikian, Gilbert. *Community 101: Reclaiming the Local Church as Community of Oneness.* Grand Rapids: Zondervan Publishing, 1997.

Bixby, Doug. *The Honest to God Church: A Pathway to God's Grace.* Herndon, Virginia: Alban Institute, 2007.

Boswell, John. *Christianity, Social Tolerance, and Homosexuality.* Chicago: University of Chicago Press, 1980.

Brawley, Robert L. ed. *Biblical Ethics and Homosexuality: Listening to Scripture.* Louisville: Westminster John Knox Press, 1996.

Brownson, James. *Bible, Gender, Sexuality: Reframing the Church's Debate on Same-Sex Relationships*. Grand Rapids: Eerdmans Publishing, 2013.

Bruckner, James K., Michelle A. Clifton-Soderstrom, and Paul E. Koptak, eds. *Living Faith: Reflection on Covenant Affirmations*. Chicago: Covenant Press, 2010.

Cannon, Justin R. *The Bible, Christianity, & Homosexuality*. Lexington: Inclusive Orthodoxy, 2009.

Campolo, Tony. "*Love the Sinner, Hate the Sin Doesn't Work.*" Red Letter Christians Blog. Accessed January 22, 2014. http://www.redletterchristians.org/lovesinner-hate-sin-doesnt-work/.

Campolo, Tony. *Red Letter Christians: A Citizen's Guide to Faith & Politics*. Ventura, California: Regal, 2008.

Chapman, Patrick M. *"Thou Shalt Not Love": What Evangelicals Really Say to Gays*. New York: Haiduk Press, 2008.

Cheng, Patrick S. *Radical Love: An Introduction to Queer Theology*. Harrisburg: Seabury Press, 2011.

Chu, Jeffrey. *Does Jesus Really Love Me?: A Gay Christian's Pilgrimage in Search of God in America*. New York: HarperCollins Publishers, 2013.

Cleveland, Christena. *Disunity in Christ: Uncovering the Hidden Forces that Keep Us Apart*. Downers Grove: Intervarsity Press, 2013.

Department of Ordered Ministry. *Baptism in the Evangelical Covenant Church*. Evangelical Covenant 113th Annual Meeting. *In Covenant Yearbook:* 1998, 388-389. Chicago: Covenant Publications, 1998.

Department of Ordered Ministry, *Policy on Baptism of the ECC*. Chicago, March 2003, http://www.covchurch.

org/resources/baptism-documents (accessed February 12, 2011).

Deymaz, Mark. *Building a Multi-Ethnic Church: Mandate, Commitments, and Practices of a Diverse Congregation.* San Francisco: Josey-Bass, 2007.

DeYoung, Curtiss Paul, Michael O. Emerson, George Yancey, and Karen Chai Kim. *United By Faith: The Multiracial Congregation as an Answer to the Problem of Race.* New York: Oxford University Press, 2003.

Duberman, Martin. *Stonewall.* New York: Plume Book, 1993.

Dunn, James D.G. *Romans 1-8. Word Biblical Commentary.* Dallas: Word Books Publisher, 1988.

Erickson, Scott E. *"Let Us Take Our Bible Seriously: The Ecclesial Nature of Biblical Interpretation." In Spirit and in Truth: Essays on Theology, Spirituality, and Embodiment in Honor of C John Weborg.* eds. Philip J. Anderson and Michelle Clifton-Soderstrom, 98-117. Chicago: Covenant Publications, 2006.

Eskridge Jr., William N. *Dishonorable Passions: Sodomy Laws in America 1861-2003.* New York: Viking Press, 2008.

Evangelical Lutheran Church in America, *A Social Statement on Human Sexuality: Gift and Trust.* Minneapolis: Augsburg Fortress Press, 2009.

Farly, Margaret. *Just Love: A Framework for Christian Sexual Ethics.* New York: Continuum International Publishing Group, 2006.

Fee, Gordon D. *The First Epistle to the Corinthians.* The New International Commentary on the New

Testament. Grand Rapids: Eerdmans Publishing Company, 1987.

Gagnon, Robert A.J. *The Bible and Homosexual Practices: Texts and Hermeneutics.* Nashville: Abingdon Press, 2001.

Gay & Lesbians Alliance Against Defamation, *GLAAD Media Reference Guide 8th Edition*, 2010, http://www.glaad.org/reference (accessed January, 26th, 2011).

Gold, Mitchell, ed. Crisis: *40 Stories Revealing the Personal, Social, and Religious Pain and Trauma of Growing up Gay in America.* Austin: Greenleaf Book Group Press, 2008.

Grenz, Stanley J. *Welcoming but not Affirming: An Evangelical Response to Homosexuality.* Louisville: Westminster John Knox Press, 1998.

Gushee, David P. *Changing our Mind.* Canton, Michigan: Read the Spirit Books, 2014.

Hays, Richard B. *The Moral Vision of the New Testament.* New York: Harper One, 1996.

Held Evans, Rachel. Keynote Speaker. Gay Christian Network Conference: Chicago, January 14th, 2014.

Helminiak, Daniel A. *What the Bible Really Says about Homosexuality.* Estancia, New Mexico: Alamo Square Press, 2000.

Hill, Wesley. *Washed and Waiting.* Grand Rapids: Zondervan, 2010.

Hirsch, Debra. *Redeeming Sex: Naked Conversations About Sexuality and Spirituality.* Downers Grove, Illinois: InterVarsity Press, 2015.

Hubbard, Thomas K. *Homosexuality in Greece and Rome.* Berkeley: University of California Press, 2003.

Jay, Karla. *Out of the Closets: Voices of the Gay Liberation*. New York: New York University Press, 1992.

Johnson, Luke Timothy. *Scripture and Discernment: Decision Making in the Church*. Nashville: Abingdon Press, 1983.

Johnson, William Stacy. *A Time to Embrace: Same-Gender Relationships in Religion, Law, and Politics*. Grand Rapids, Michigan: Eerdmans Publishing Company, 2006.

Keller, Timothy. *Center Church: Doing Balanced Gospel-Centered Ministry in Your City*. Grand Rapids: Zondervan, 2012.

Kinnaman, David. *You Lost Me: Why Young Christians are Leaving Church...and Rethinking Faith*. Grand Rapids: Baker Books, 2011.

Kinnaman, David. *UnChristian*. Grand Rapids: Baker Books, 2007.

Knust, Jennifer. *Unprotected Texts: The Bible's Surprising Contradictions about Sex and Desire*. New York: Harper One, 2011.

Lee, Justin. *Torn: Rescuing the Gospel from the Gays-vs.-Christians Debate*. New York: Jericho Books, 2012.

Loader, William. *The New Testament on Sexuality*. Grand Rapids, Michigan: Eerdmans Publishing Company, 2012.

Marin, Andrew. *Love is an Orientation: Elevating the Conversation with the Gay Community*. Downers Grove: Intervarsity Press, 2009.

Martin, Dale B. *Sex and the Single Savior: Gender and Sexuality in Biblical Interpretation*. Louisville: Westminster John Knox Press, 2006.

McNeill, John J. *The Church and the Homosexual.* Boston: Beacon Press, 1976.

McNeill, John. *Taking a Chance on God.* Boston: Beacon Press, 1988.

Merton, Thomas. *Life and Holiness.* Image: The Abbey of Gethesemani Inc., 1963.

Miner, Jeff and John Tyler Connoley. *The Children are Free.* Indianapolis: Found Pearl Press, 2008.

Myers, Bryant L. *Walking with the Poor: Principles and Practices of Transformational Development.* New York: Orbis Books, 1999.

Nelson, Arthur A. R. *Prayers Public and Personal.* Chicago: Covenant Press, 2010.

Nussbaum, Martha C. *From Disgust to Humanity: Sexual Orientation & Constitutional Law.* Oxford: Oxford University Press, 2010.

Peterson, Judy. "Community" *Pastor Judy's Blog.* http://northpark/typepad.com/pastor_judys_blog/2010/10/community.html (accessed October 20, 2010).

Piazza, Michael S. *Gay by God: How to be Lesbian or Gay and Christian.* Dallas: Hope Publishing, 1994.

Rogers, Jack. *Jesus, the Bible and Homosexuality: Explode the Myths, Heal the Church.* Louisville: Westminster John Knox Press, 2009.

Rooker, Mark F. Leviticus. *The New American Commentary.* Nashville: Broadman & Holman Publishers, 2000.

de Rossi, Portia. *Unbearable Lightness.* New York: Atria Books, 2010.

Rutledge, Leigh W. *The Gay Decades.* New York: Plume Books, 1992.

Schaefer, Franklyn. *Defrocked: How a Father's Act of Love Shook the United Methodist Church.* St. Louis, Missouri: Chalice Press, 2014.

Scroggs, Robin. *The New Testament and Homosexuality.* Philadelphia: Fortress Press, 1983.

Seow, Choon-Leong. *Homosexuality and Christian Community.* Louisville: Westminster John Knox Press, 1996.

Serano, Julia. *Whipping Girl.* Berkeley: Seal Press, 1997.

Smith, David Livingstone. *Less Than Human: Why We Demean, Enslave, and Exterminate Others.* New York: St. Martin's Griffin, 2011.

Spencer, F. Scott, "Eunuchs," in *Eerdmans Dictionary of the Bible*, ed. David Noel Freedman. Grand Rapids: Eerdmans Publishing Group, 2000.

Spencer, Michael. *Mere Churchianity.* Colorado Springs: Water Brook Press, 2010.

Soards, Marion L. *Scripture and Homosexuality: Biblical Authority and the Church Today.* Louisville: Westminster John Knox Press, 1995.

Sullivan, Andrew. *Virtually Normal: An Argument about Homosexuality.* New York: Vintage Books, 1996.

Tickle, Phyllis. *The Great Emergence.* Grand Rapids: Baker Books, 2008.

Trembling Before G-D, DVD, documentary directed by Sandi Simcha DuBowski. Israel: Simba Leib Productions, 2001.

Via, Dan O. and Robert A.J. Gagnon. *Homosexuality and the Bible: Two Views*. Minneapolis: Fortress Press, 2003.

Vines, Matthew. *God and the Gay Christian: The Biblical Case in Support of Same-Sex Relationships*. New York: Convergent Publishing, 2014.

Webb, William J. *Slaves, Women & Homosexuals: Exploring the Hermeneutics of Cultural Analysis*. Downers Grove: InterVarsity Press, 2001.

Wenham, Gordon J. *Genesis 16-50*. Word Biblical Commentary. Dallas: Word Books, 1994.

White, Mel. *Strangers at the Gate*. New York: Plume Books, 1995.

Wilson, Ken. *A Letter to My Congregation: An Evangelical Pastor's Path to Embracing People Who Are Gay, Lesbian, and Transgender into the Community of Jesus*. Canton, Michigan: Read the Spirit Books, 2014.

Wink, Walter ed. *Homosexuality and Christian Faith: Questions of Conscience for the Churches*. Minneapolis: Fortress Press, 1999.

Wold, Donald J. *Out of Order: Homosexuality in the Bible and the Ancient Near East*. Grand Rapids: Baker Books, 1998.

Wright, Chely. *Like Me*. New York: Pantheon Books, 2010.

Wright, NT. *Paul and Faithfulness of God*. Minneapolis: Fortress Press, 2013.

ENDNOTES

1   Some names of personal friends have been changed to protect their identity and privacy.
2   1 John 4:18
3   Many gay individuals secretly struggle with their sexual identity throughout their teen years. Many, I've learned, battle with internal homophobia and self-hatred, and even contemplate suicide when they come to realize their orientation.
4   Nathan Albert. "I Hugged a Man in His Underwear. And I am Proud." *It Seems to Me...*, accessed January 25, 2014. http://naytinalbert.blogspot.com/2010/06/i-hugged-man-in-his-underwear-and-i-am.html. The post was edited for typos.
5   Jack Shepherd. "21 Pictures That Will Restore Your Faith In Humanity." Buzzfeed. Accessed November 23, 2013. http://www.buzzfeed.com/expresident/pictures-that-will-restore-your-faith-in-humanity
6   For more, see the I'm Sorry page on The Marin Foundation's website: themarinfoundation.org/imsorry.
7   Tristan Ongenae. Persona e-mail communication with the author, in its original form. June 2010.
8   Again, see The Marin Foundation's "I'm Sorry Campaign." themarinfoundation.org/imsorry.
9   1 Peter 2:4-5
10 John 13:35
11 I have been using the terminology "Belong, Believe, Behave" for the last few years. However,

Doug Bixby, in his wonderful book *The Honest to God Church: A Pathway to God's Grace* (Herndon, Virginia: the Alban Institute, 2007) uses the phrase "Belong, Believe, Become." I have adopted my phrasing due to this book. Phyllis Tickle also uses this language in her *The Great Emergence: How Christianity is Changing and Why* (Grand Rapids: Baker Books, 2008).

12   2 Corinthians 5:18-19

13   John 13:1-17, Luke 7:36-50, Mark 14 and Matthew 23:25-28 are just a few references.

14   John 20:27

15   John 20:28

16   Andrew Marin, *Love is an Orientation* (Downers Grove: Intervarsity Press, 2009), 22.

17   There are countless other autobiographies that allow readers to get a glimpse of experiences of those individuals in the LGBT community. Highly recommended readings include: Mel White, *Strangers at the Gate* (New York: Plume Books, 1995); *Wesley Hill, Washed and Waiting* (Grand Rapids: Zondervan, 2010); Chely Wright, *Like Me* (New York: Pantheon Books, 2010); Portia de Rossi, *Unbearable Lightness* (New York: Atria Books, 2010); Julia Serano, *Whipping Girl* (Berkeley: Seal Press, 1997); Jay Karla, *Out of the Closets: Voices of the Gay Liberation* (New York: New York University Press, 1992); Mitchell Gold, ed., *Crisis: 40 Stories Revealing the Personal, Social, and Religious Pain and Trauma of Growing up Gay in America* (Austin: Greenleaf Book Group Press, 2008).

18   Martin Duberman, *Stonewall* (New York: Plume Book, 1993), 182-185.

19   Ibid., 193.

20   Leigh W. Rutledge, *The Gay Decades* (New York: Plume Books, 1992), 1-3.

21   Ibid., 21.

22   Ibid., 61.

23   Ibid., 96-97, 104.

24   William N. Eskridge Jr., *Dishonorable Passions: Sodomy Laws in America* 1861-2003 (New York: Viking Press, 2008), 10-12.

25   Marin, *Love is an Orientation*, 38.

26   For more, see Tony Campolo's interview for the New Direction DVD. "Love the Sinner, Hate the Sin Doesn't Work." Red Letter Christians Blog. Accessed January 22, 2014. http://www.redletter-christians.org/love-sinner-hate-sin-doesntwork/

27   Using the term *homosexuality* is not the same as labeling an individual a *homosexual*. I am arguing that the latter is harmful.

28   For a great treatment on this topic, I encourage you to read Tim Keller's *Center Church: Doing Balanced Gospel-Centered Ministry in Your City* (Grand Rapids: Zondervan, 2012).

29   For more on this, please reference chapters 3-6 in my thesis *Belong, Believe, Become: The Evangelical Covenant Church and Homosexuality* (Chicago: North Park Theological Seminary, 2011), which is available for download.

30   Donald J. Wold, *Out of Order: Homosexuality in the Bible and the Ancient Near East* (Grand Rapids: Baker Books, 1998), 80.

31   See Gen. 4:1, 17, 25, 19:18, 24:16, 38:26; Judg. 11:39, 19:25; 1 Sam. 1:19; and 1 Kings 1:4.

32   Gordan J. Wenham, *Genesis 16-50 Word Biblical Commentary* (Dallas: Word Books, 1994), 55

33   Stanley J. Grenz, *Welcoming but not Affirming: An Evangelical Response to Homosexuality* (Louisville: Westminster John Knox Press, 1998), 37.

34   Robert A.J. Gagnon, *The Bible and Homosexual Practice: Texts and Hermeneutics* (Nashville: Abingdon Press, 2001), 75-76.

35   Jack Rogers, *Jesus, the Bible, and Homosexuality: Explore the Myths, Heal the Church* (Louisville: Westminster John Knox Press, 2009), 67.

36   See Deut. 29:23, 32:32; Isa. 3:9, 13:19; Jer. 23:14, 49:18; Lam. 4:6; Ezek. 16:46-48; Amos 4:11; Zeph. 2:9; Matt. 10:15; Luke 17:29; Rom. 9:29; 2 Pet. 2:6; and Jude 7.

37   Rogers, *Jesus, the Bible, and Homosexuality*, 68.

38   Marion L. Soards. *Scripture and Homosexuality: Biblical Authority and the Church Today* (Louisville: Westminster John Knox Press, 1995), 16.

39   Mark F. Rooker, *Leviticus*, The New American Commentary (Nashville: Broadman & Holman Publishers, 2000), 246.

40   Choon-Leong Seow, *Homosexuality and Christian Community* (Louisville: Westminster John Knox Press, 1996), 19. See also, Klyne Snodgrass, *Divorce and Remarriage, Occasional Paper* (Chicago: Covenant Press, 1989).

41   David Helminiak, *What the Bible Really Says About Homosexuality* (New Mexico: Alamo Square Press, 2000), 64.

42   Dan O. Via and Robert A. J. Gagnon, *Homosexuality and the Bible: Two Views* (Minneapolis: Fortress Press, 2000), 6-8.

43   For more, see Gagnon, *Bible and Homosexual Practice*, 263 and Hays, *The Moral Vision*, 385.

44   Gagnon, *Bible and Homosexual Practice*, 267-268.

45 Robin Scroggs. *The New Testament and Homosexuality* (Philadelphia: Fortress Press, 1983), 24-25.

46 Ibid., 36-37.

47 Ibid., 38.

48 Richard B. Hays, *The Moral Vision of the New Testament* (New York: Harper One, 1996), 116.

49 Helminiak, *What the Bible Really Says About Homosexuality*, 78.

50 John Boswell, *Christianity, Social Tolerance, and Homosexuality* (Chicago: University of Chicago Press, 1980), 79.

51 James V. Brownson, *Bible, Gender, Sexuality: Reframing the Church's Debate on Same-Sex Relationships* (Grand Rapids: Eerdmans Publishing Company, 2013), 201-202.

52 Ibid., 164, 177-178.

53 Ibid., 228-229, 245, 255.

54 Ibid., 232-237, 245, 255.

55 Ibid., 237-245, 255.

56 Hays, *The Moral Vision*, 382.

57 For more, see Brownson, *Bible, Gender, Sexuality*, 42-43.

58 Ibid., 40.

59 Wold, *Out of Order*, 190-191.

60 Gordon D. Fee, *The First Epistle to the Corinthians*, The New International Commentary on the New Testament (Grand Rapids: Eerdmans Publishing Company, 1987), 243

61 Dale B. Martin, *Sex and the Single Savior: Gender and Sexuality in Biblical Interpretation* (Louisville: Westminster Knoxville Press, 2006), 44.

62 Ibid., 44-45.

63 Ibid., 101.

64 You can see this in reference to divorce in Matthew 19 and Mark 10 as well as references to sexual sinners in John 4; 7-8 and Luke 7.

65 *Trembling Before G-D*, DVD, directed by Sandi Simcha DuBowski. Simba Leib Productions, 2001.

66 David Livingstone Smith. *Less Than Human: Why We Demean, Enslave, and Exterminate Others* (New York: St. Martin's Griffin, 2011), 4, 25, 13.

67 Genesis 1:26-27

68 Genesis 1:31

69 Genesis 3:5

70 Genesis 3:12-13

71 Much of this is influenced by my reading of Gilbert Bilezikian's *Community 101: Reclaiming the Local Church as Community of Oneness.* (Grand Rapids: Zondervan Publishing, 1997).

72 Genesis 2:19-20

73 Thomas Merton. *Life and Holiness* (Image: The Abbey of Gethesemani, Inc, 1963), 87.

74 Bilezikian *Community 101*, 51.

75 Proverbs 6:16

76 See Proverbs 6:19

77 2 Timothy 2:14

78 Bilezikian *Community 101*, 60.

79 1 Corinthians 3:16-17

80 Bilezikian *Community 101*, 37.

81 John 17:20-23

82 For a great look at this prayer of Jesus in relation to creating unity in multi-ethnic church communities, read Mark Deymaz's *Building a Multi-Ethnic Church: Mandate, Commitments, and Practices of a Diverse Congregation* (San Francisco: Josey-Bass, 2007), 9-11, as well as Curtiss Paul DeYoung, Michael O. Emerson, George

Yancey, and Karen Chai Kim's *United By Faith: The Multiracial Congregation as an Answer to the Problem of Race* (New York: Oxford University Press, 2003).

83 Ephesians 5:26-27

84 While working at The Marin Foundation, we frequently used the language of "holy moments." It was first publicly referenced in The Marin Foundation's DVD Curriculum *Love is an Orientation* (Grand Rapids: Zondervan, 2011) and my blog post, *When Your Child Comes Out* on the Patheos blog.

85 Although an incredibly well known and powerful story in the Gospel of John, most early manuscripts do not have this section and it is questioned whether this should be included within the text.

86 John 8:11

87 The above prayer was presented in an edited form in Arthur A.R. Nelson, *Prayers Public and Personal* (Chicago: Covenant Press, 2010).

CPSIA information can be obtained
at www.ICGtesting.com
Printed in the USA
BVOW09s0408290417
482523BV00002B/297/P

9 781942 011293